C

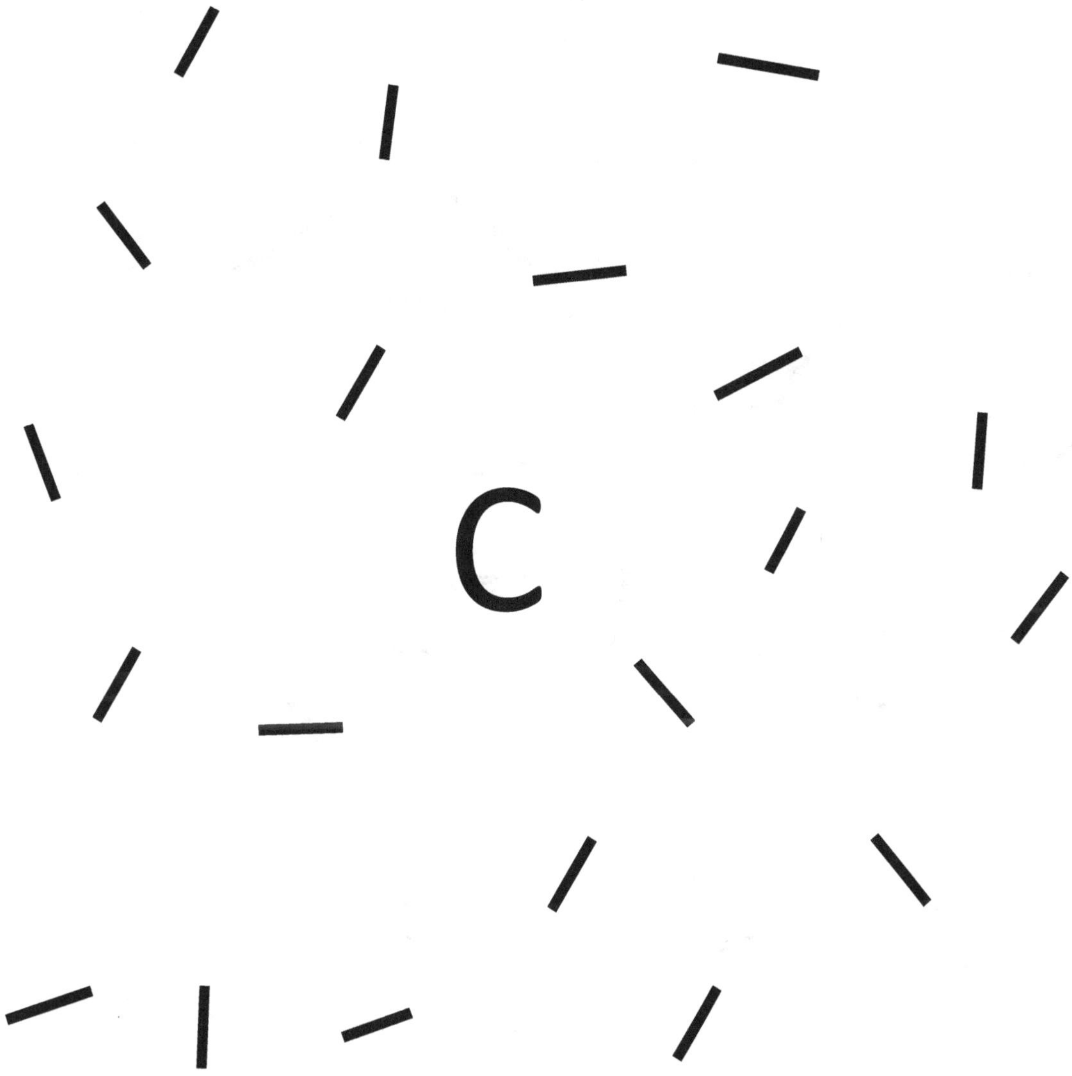

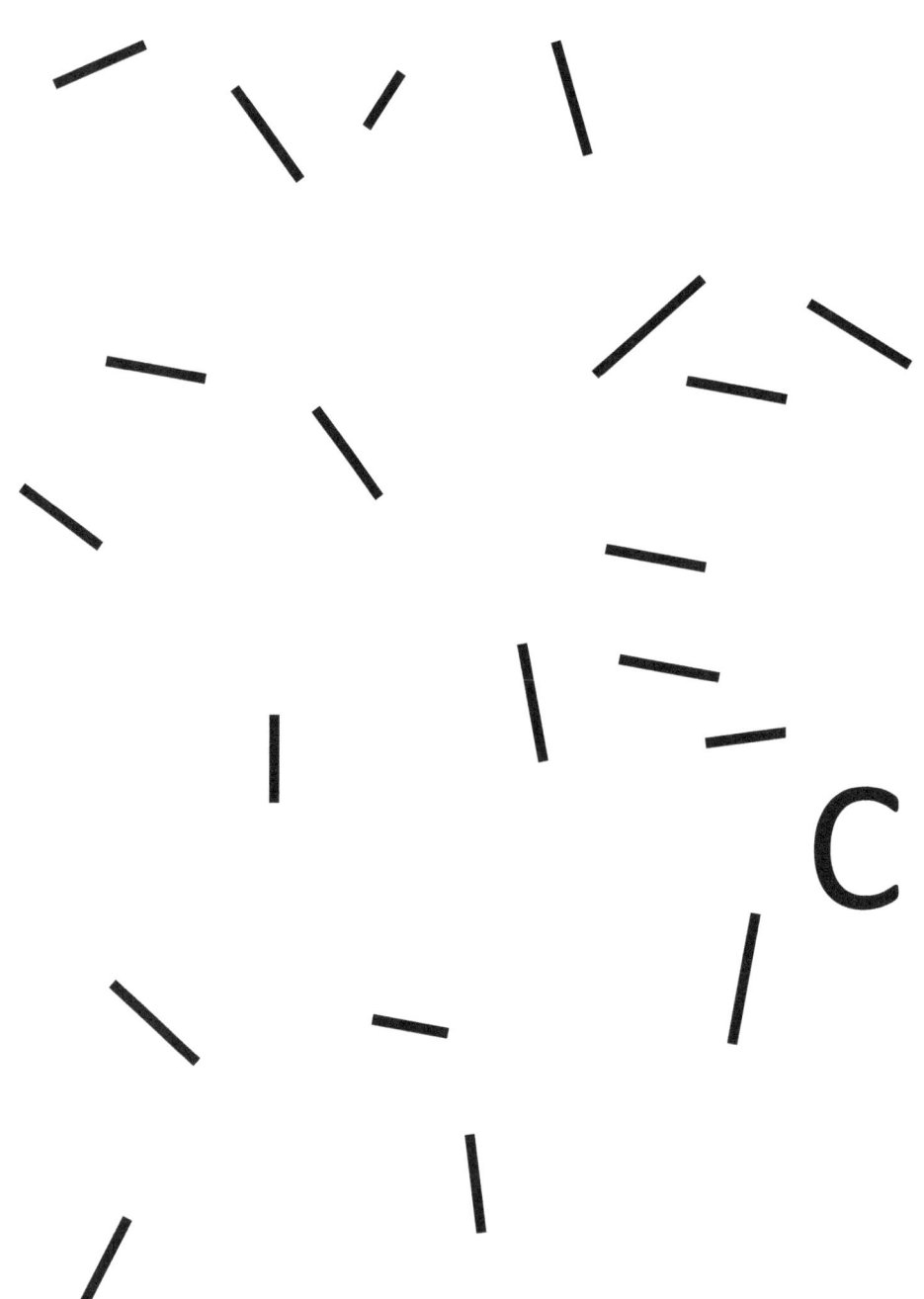

C

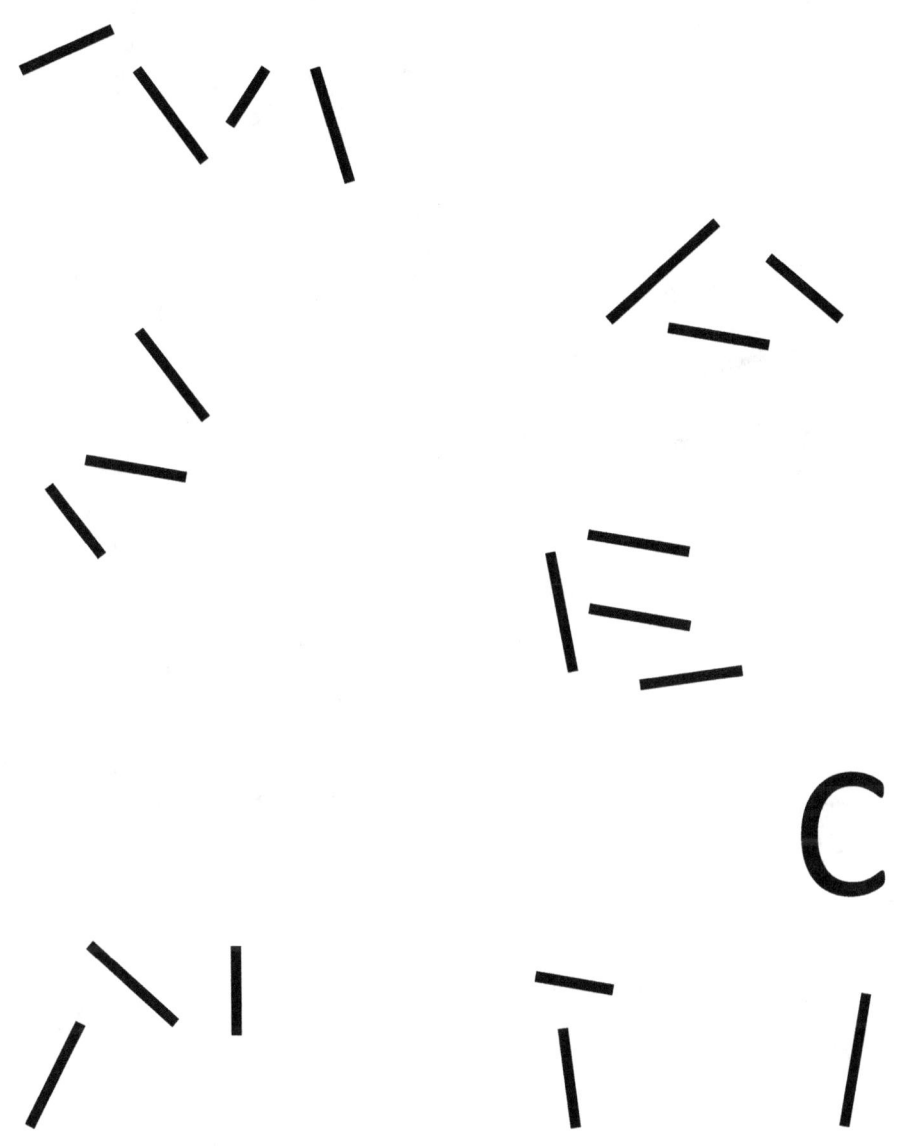

C

M

N

G

E

A

N

I

M

N

N

G

E

A

N

I

I M A G I N E

M N G E N A I

MEANING

AND
MORALITY

We are facing a crisis of meaning and morality.

MEANING AND MORALITY
A crisis of meaning originates in our use of language.

Language is the basis of most human thought. And the primary unit of language is the word.

A word is an "atom" in the universe of language. It is a particle of meaning so small that it admits to no division.

A crisis of meaning originates when a people who share a common language begin to use the same word to indicate different concepts. Not just variations of the same concept, not just different slants on the same idea, but truly different ideas called by the same word.

Gender, male, female, marriage. Diversity, equality, liberty.

This state of affairs profoundly impacts communication. Communication is not simply the exchange of information. Communication is, at its heart, shared comprehension.

A crisis of meaning leads to the destruction of shared comprehension.

When we talk of an individual human being, there is little confusion about the object to which we refer. But when we speak of things like liberty or equality, we are referring to relationships between individual human beings. And these relationships are frequently the result of rules, or the lack of the them, that influence and guide human behavior.

A crisis of morality originates in the disruption of rules that guide human behavior.

As the rules that guide human behavior break down among a people who share a common set of rules, the social order becomes transformed. And it, too, can break down.

Even if all the elements of a social system, all the individual human beings who comprise a social system, remain exactly the same, as the rules of conduct change, so does the social order.

A crisis of morality leads to the destruction of a social order.

THE INDIVIDUAL
Each of us are born unique, with feelings and thoughts that exist, in the beginning, within for each individual to experience.

Each and every one of us is born naked and alone. Vulnerable. Not a penny to our name. No clothes. No possessions. Homeless. Speechless. And powerless.

We are each born into *situations* and *circumstances* beyond our control, situations and circumstances born of pure luck, good or bad or both, and the *opportunities* that greet each and every individual are *as different as the individuals themselves.*

LIBERTY AND EQUALITY
Some of us were fortunate enough to be born into a social system rooted in individual human liberty and equality.

Individual liberty and equality are not qualities intrinsic to a group of individual human beings because of the way those individuals think and feel about each other.

Individual liberty and equality are functions of the rules by which a group of individual human beings operate.

Individual liberty and equality are characterized by a certain set of rules that govern human behavior.

In a society whose *growth* has been *fueled* by a *morality* grounded in *concepts of individual liberty* and the *notion of equality* among innumerable unique individual human beings, a *crisis of morality* can lead to the *destruction* of individual liberty and equality.

THESE SONGS
These songs sing of meaning and morality.

They sing of shared comprehension. They sing of human feeling and thought, individuality, family, community, and society. They sing of the *difference between* creating equality among a group of unique individuals *or* making all those unique individuals average in the name of equality. They sing of time. They sing of the growth of the individual. They sing of love and the bonds between individuals. They sing of good and evil. They sing of knowledge. They sing of the milieu from which individual liberty and equality arises.

They sing of human beings living life together.

The Songs
If I Found
Blind Men
Mediocre Town
Pretty Little Angel
Cultural Prescription
Ol' John Henry
Not Something I Saw
The Establishment
Gliding on a Rainbow
Georgie
Loyal Disrespect
Her Sweet Shoulder

PICTURES

When words fail us, we can resort to pictures.
Representation by presentation.
Seeing is believing.
Songs in the key of see.

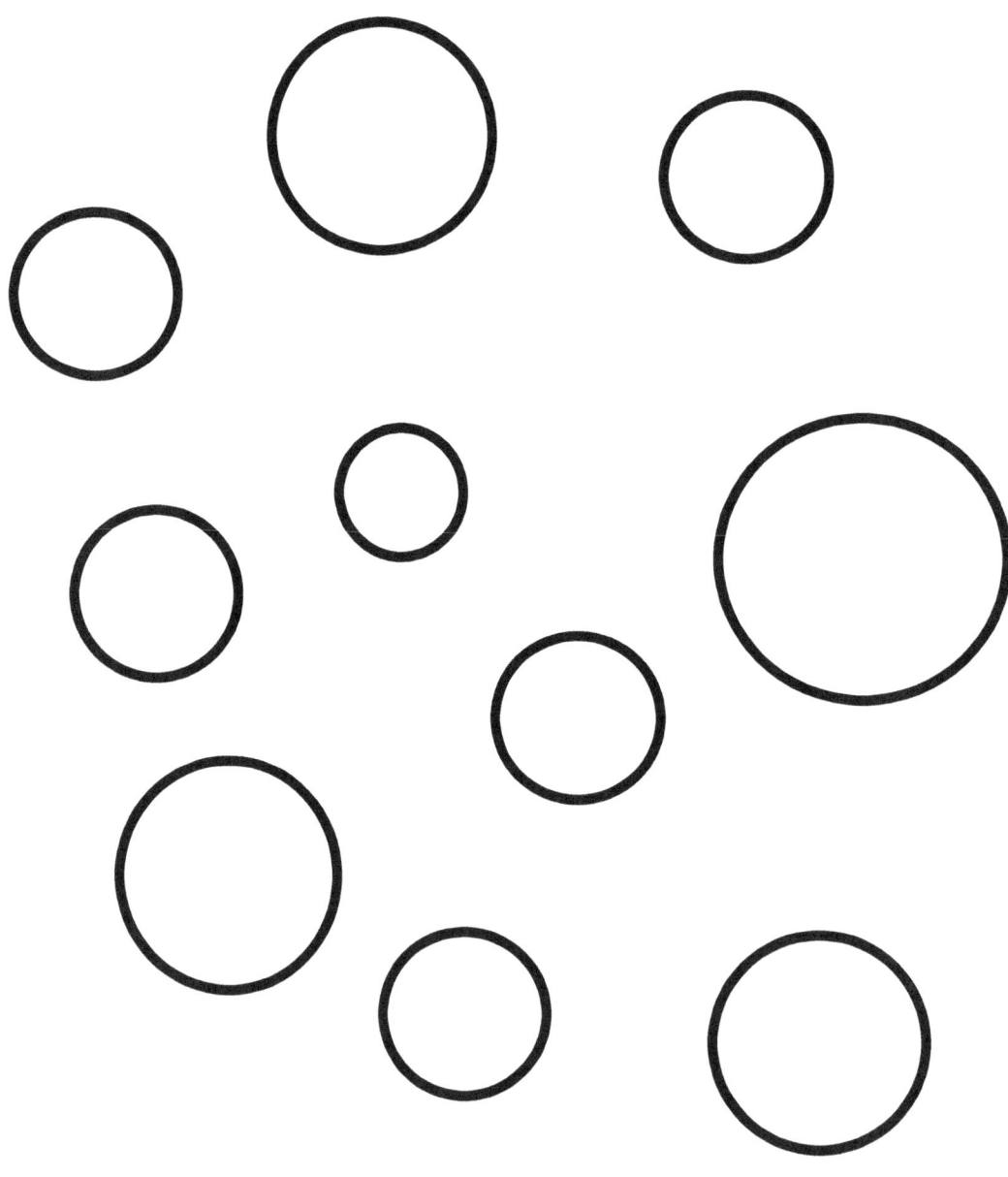

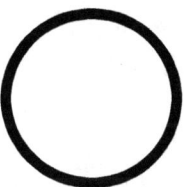

If I Found

If I found her
Who thought like that
Would walk and talk and felt like that

Alive as the sky
And deep as the sea
Would wander with time
So gracefully

If I found
That she did live and breathe
And lived and laughed
So gloriously

Would that be love?
Would that be me?
And would we live
Separately

Blind Men at Work

There are blind men at work
Working every day
Working minutes, hours
Working for good pay.

There are blind men at work
At jobs that require sight
Laughing away the daytime
And wasting time at night.

Their cause is a noble one
And they all have good hearts
But even working hard
They'll only do a part.

'Cause they're blind men.
Blind men.

Can't work in this world
On things that you just don't see
Can't work on answers
To questions unknown to me.

Can't work with the future
Until it's made known
Can't work with time
Until you feel it growing.

There are blind men at work
Workin' oh so hard
Let's give them something
So we all can do our part.

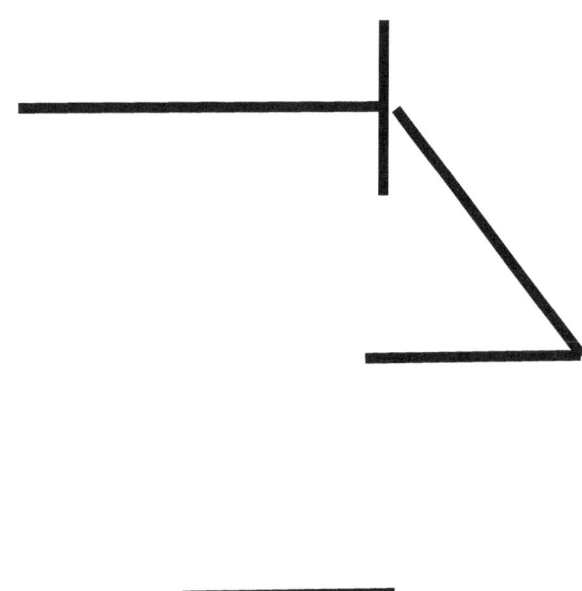

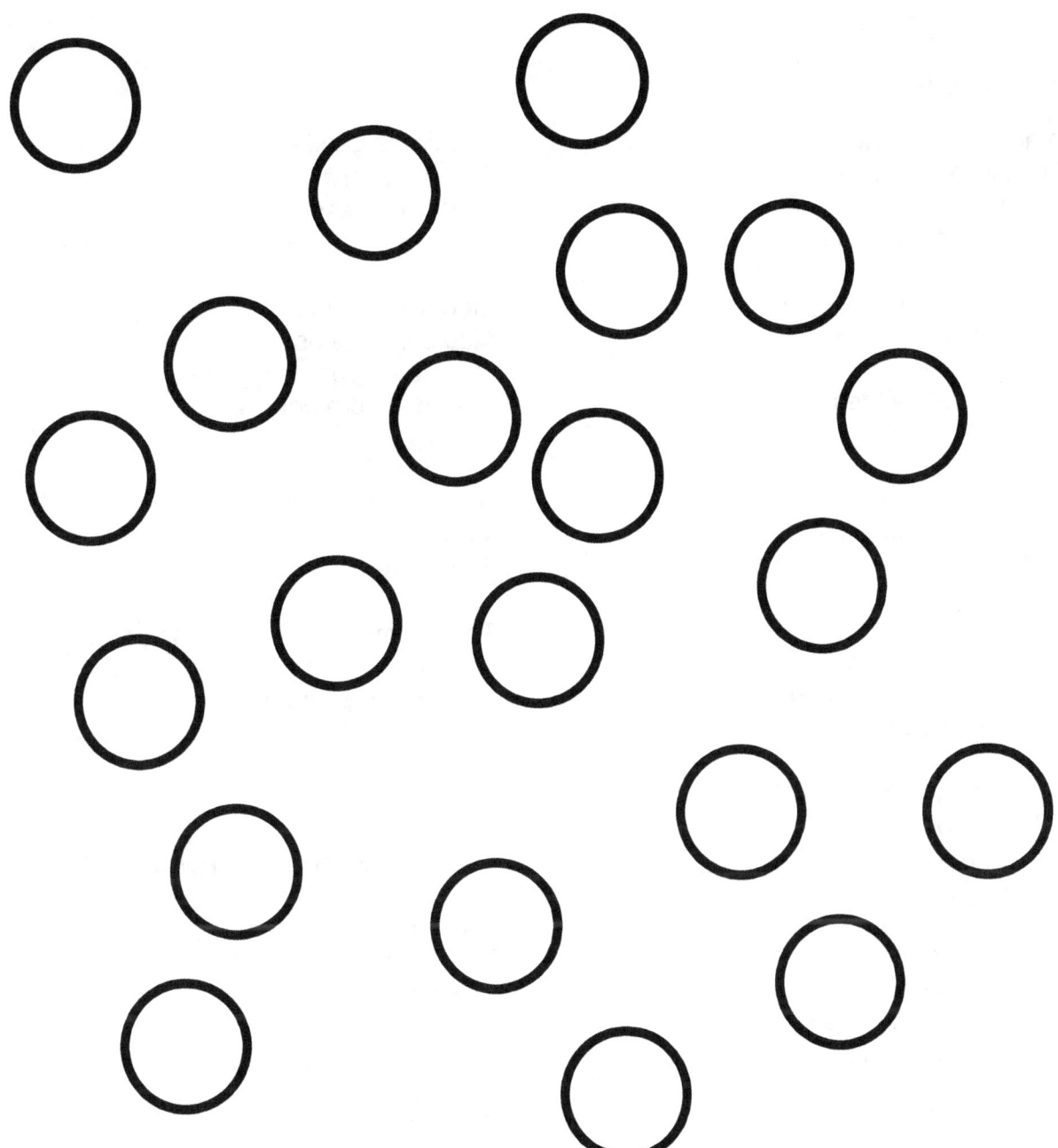

Mediocre Town

In a mediocre town
Filled with mediocre men
Playing mediocre games
With mediocre friends

Live some mediocre guys
With mediocre eyes
Telling mediocre lies
Over mediocre fries.

Dating mediocre gals
Making mediocre vows
Raising mediocre kids
And families.

Live in mediocre homes
On mediocre streets
Lined by mediocre shrubs
And mediocre trees.

Mediocre rooms
With mediocre floors
Mediocre windows
And mediocre doors.

Mediocre walls
Mediocre halls
Mediocre cellphones
And mediocre calls.

Driving mediocre vans
Getting mediocre tans
Mediocre toys and candies

Mediocre schools
Mediocre rules
Mediocre songs
'Bout where we all belong.

Mediocre good deeds
And mediocre sins
Mediocre losses
And mediocre wins.

Mediocre smiles
Mediocre frowns
Mediocre caps
And mediocre gowns.

Mediocre feeling
Mediocre thought
Mediocre things
That were just bought.

Then comes a noble, young soul
With higher goals
Looking for something
That just ain't sold.

Looks over here
Looks over there
Looking and looking everywhere.

In this mediocre town
Filled with mediocre men
Playing mediocre jokes
On mediocre friends

Mediocre guys
With mediocre eyes
Telling mediocre lies
Over hot apple pie.

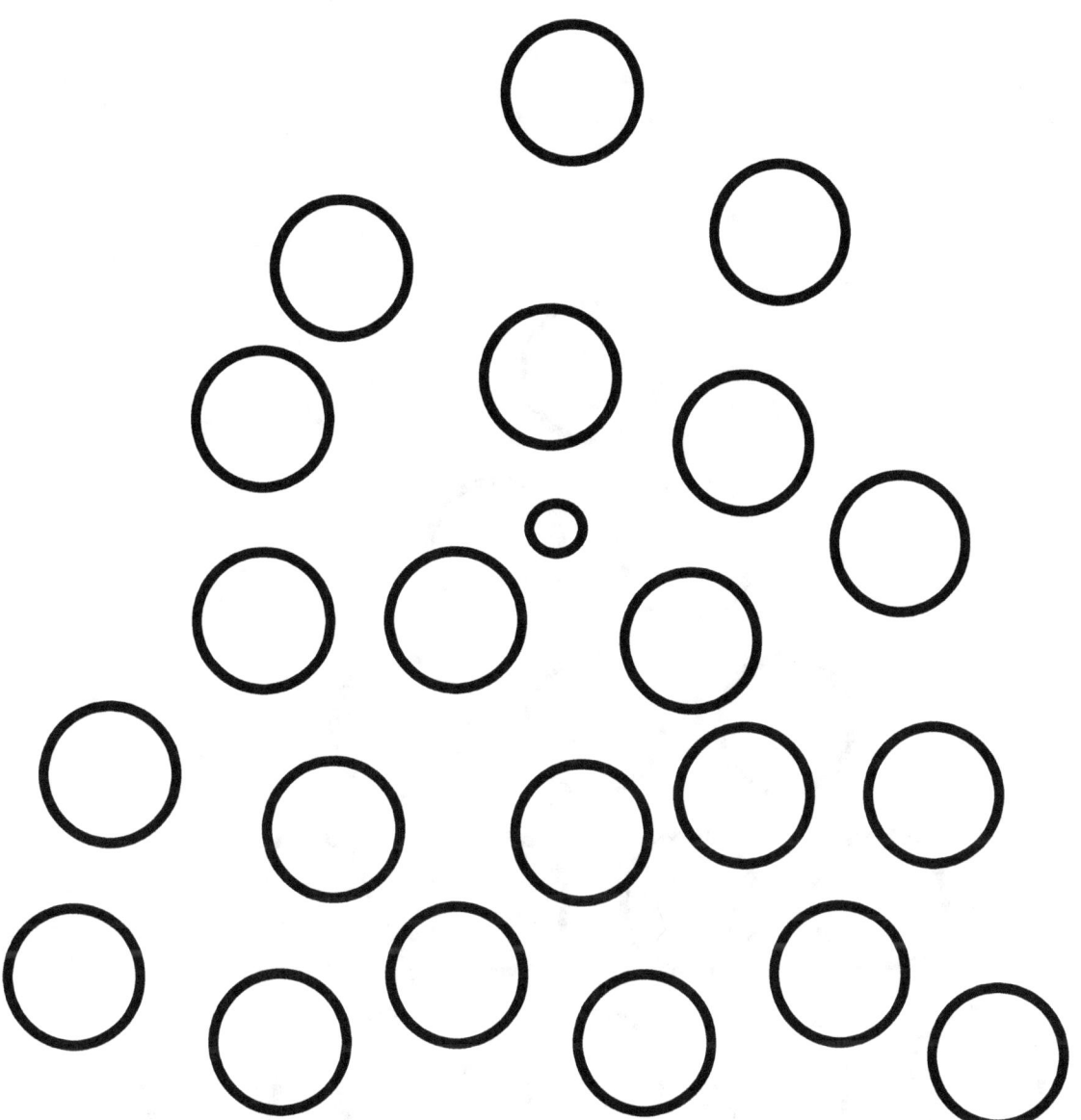

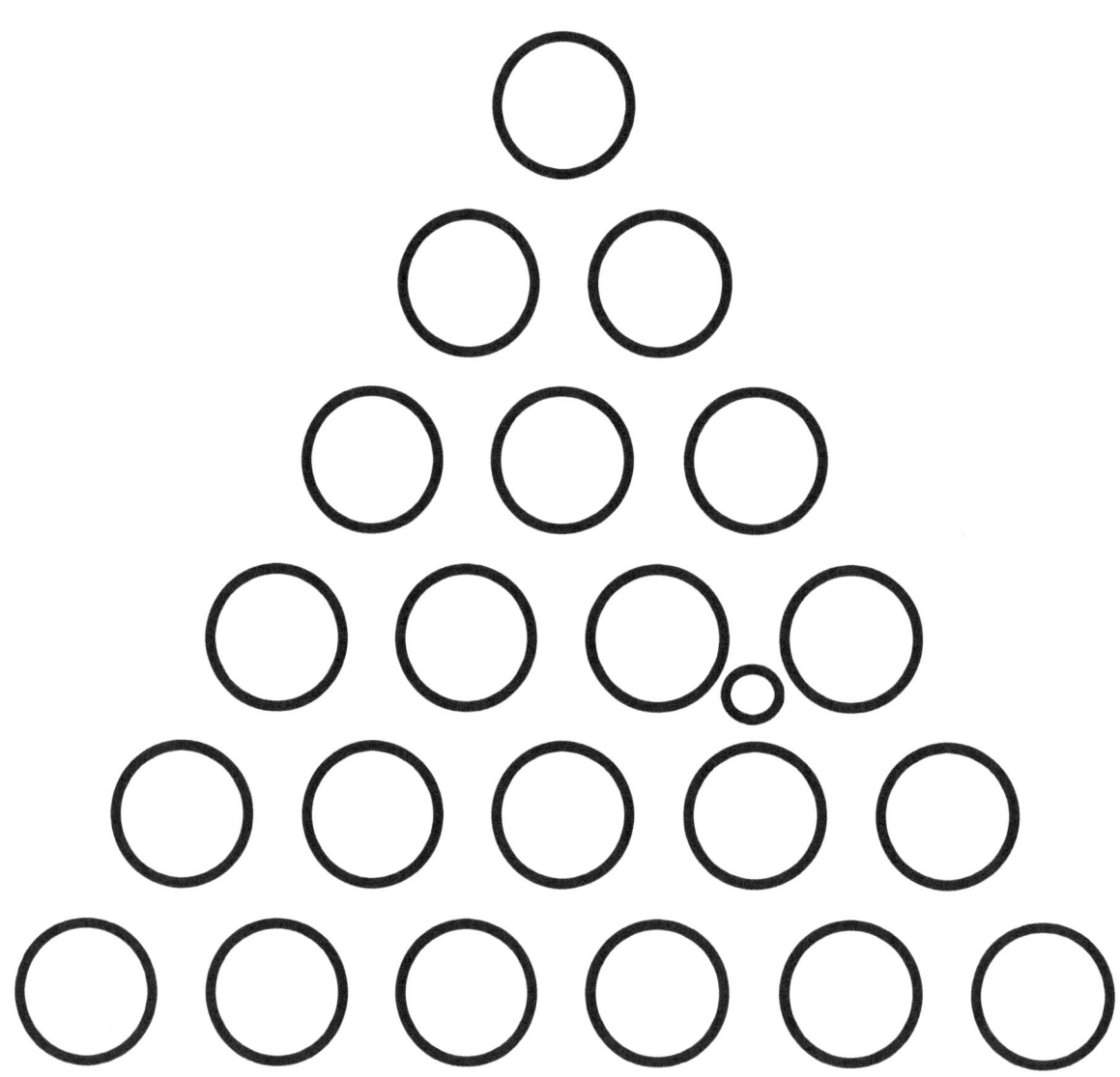

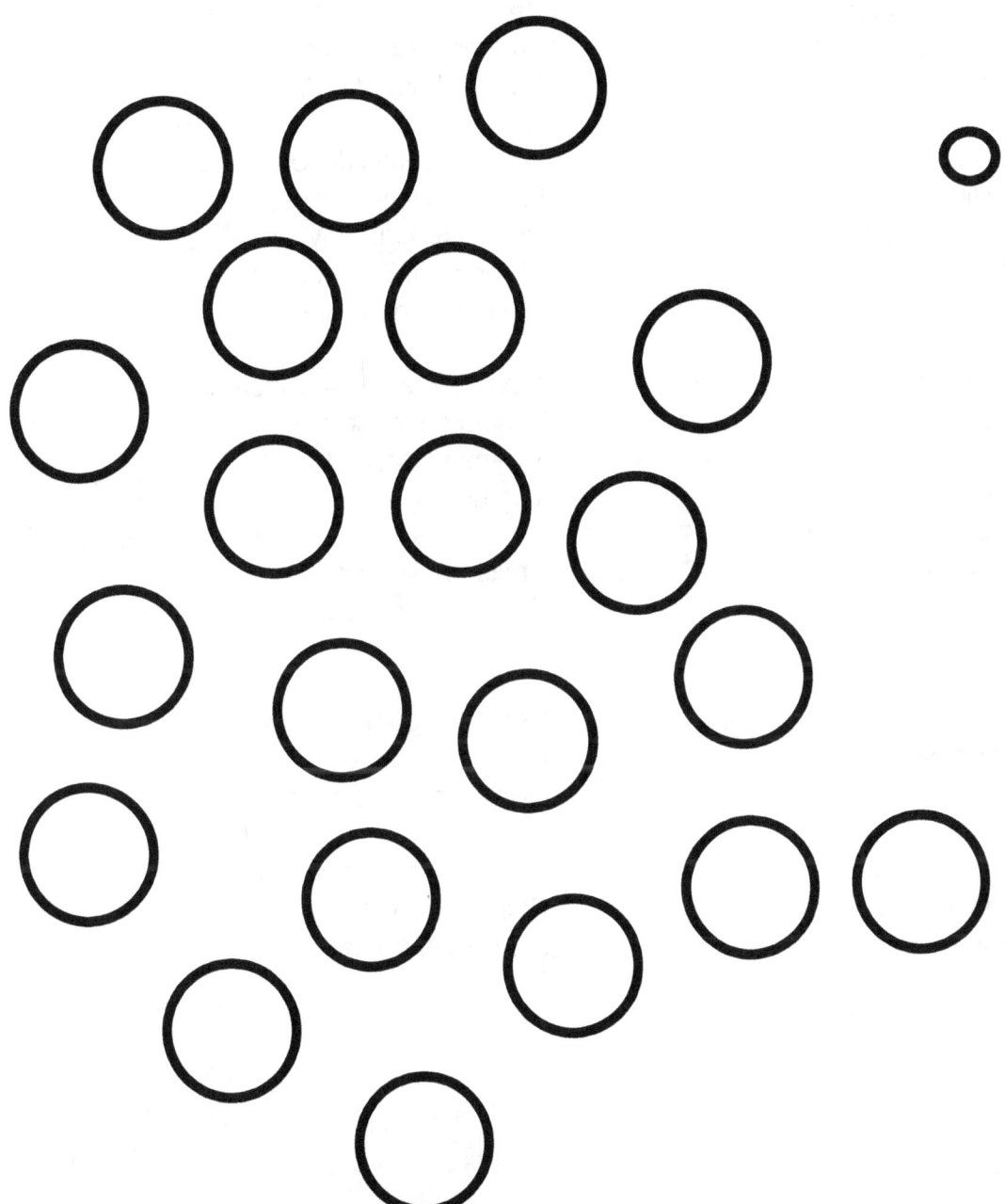

23

Pretty Little Angel

I had a pretty little angel
I had a pretty little angel
She stepped out of a dream
Walked into my life
Stepped out of a dream.

I had a pretty little angel
I had a pretty little angel
She walked into my life
Stepped out of a dream
Walked into my life.

Now she means so much to me
Means so much to me
Means so much to me
Yes she does
She always seems to make me
Smile, smile, smile
Oh, yes, she does
And she will.

Now she's come and gone
She's far from home
Gone, gone, gone, gone

Now she's on her own and
Roams, roams, roams
In her own home.

I had a pretty little angel
I had a pretty little angel
He stepped out of a dream
Walked into my life
Stepped out of a dream.

I had a pretty little angel
I had a pretty little angel
He walked into my life
Stepped out of a dream
Walked into my life.

Now he means so much to me
Means so much to me
Means so much to me
Yes he does
He always seems to make me
Smile, smile, smile
Oh, yes, he does
And he will.

Now he's come and gone
He's far from home
Gone, gone, gone, gone

Now he's on his own and
Roams, roams, roams
In his own home.

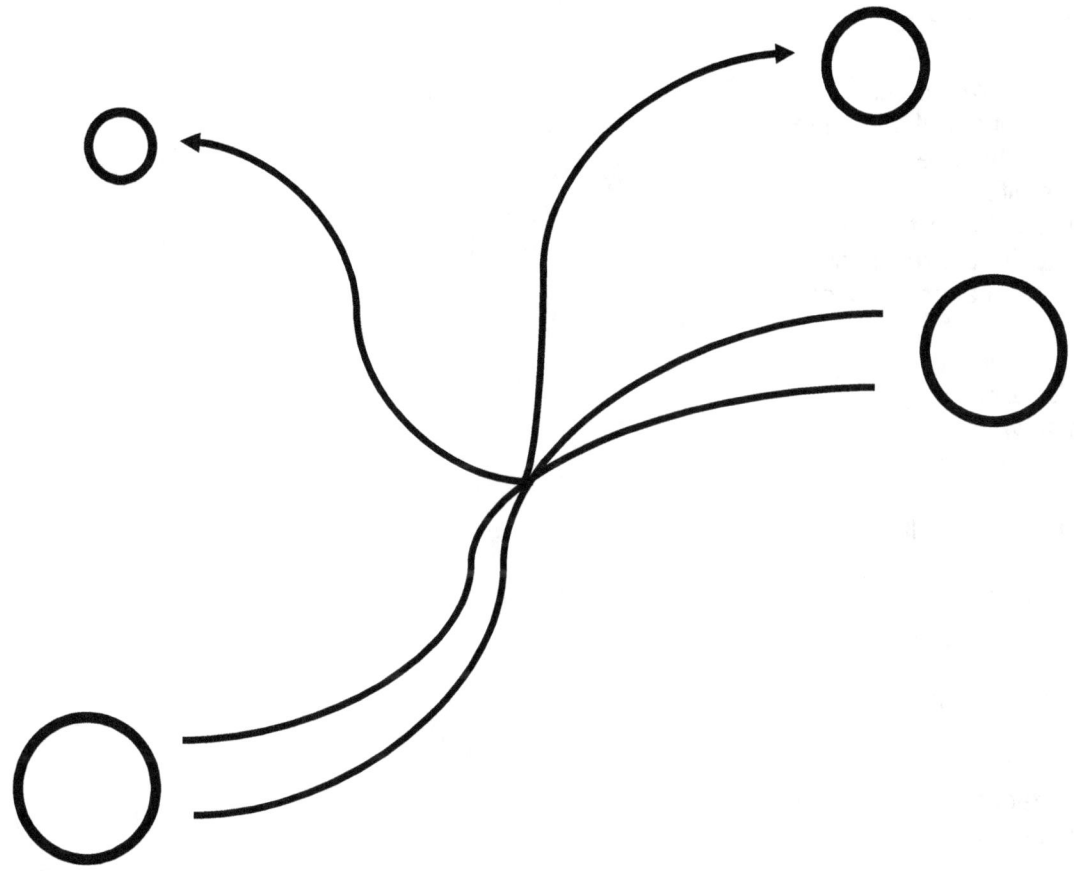

Cultural Prescription

Well the gang's all down
At the local corner parlor
Laughing with each other
'Bout the local food and barber

Some new folk walk in
From a little further farther
Need something more
Need something strong
Need to feel a life
Where we all belong

Need a cultural prescription
Need to feel about something
We all can believe in
A spirit of life
We all live alive with
Need a cultural prescription
Need a cultural prescription.

Well the gang's all down
At the local corner parlor
Laughing with each other
'Bout the local food and barber

Some new folk walk in
From a little further farther
Need something more
Need something strong
Need to feel a life
Where we all belong

Need a cultural prescription
Need to feel about something
We all can agree on
A spirit of life
We all live alive with

Need a cultural prescription
Cultural prescription.

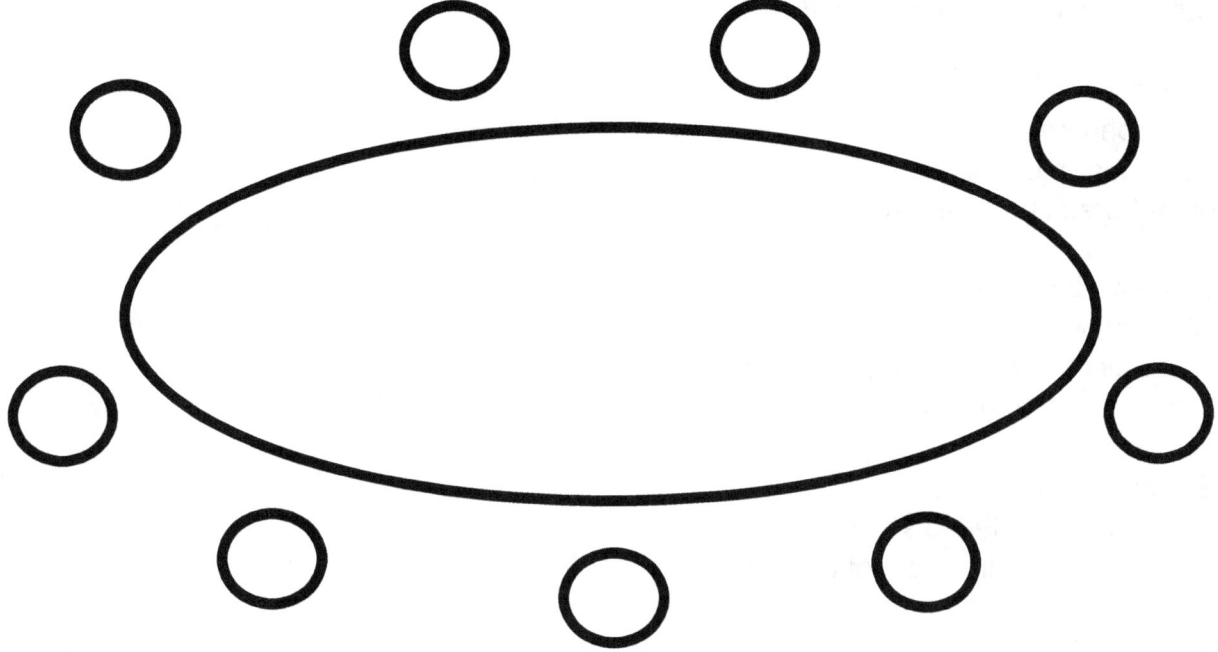

Ol' John Henry

Ol' John Henry
Had gone to school
Ostensibly to learn
But his mind had been abused

That school was good
This John knew
But to learn to think
Meant breaking some rules.

So there John sat
With his philosophy
And while his teachers taught facts
John sought meaning

General propositions
He for sure wanted to know
But it was the framework of thought
That he wondered about.
And he thought.

Simple minded people
They do simple minded things
All day.
All day, all day, all day.
All day, all day.

Simple minded people
They do simple minded things
All day.
All day, all day, all day.
All day, all day.

Show me a simple man
And I'll show you a simple way.

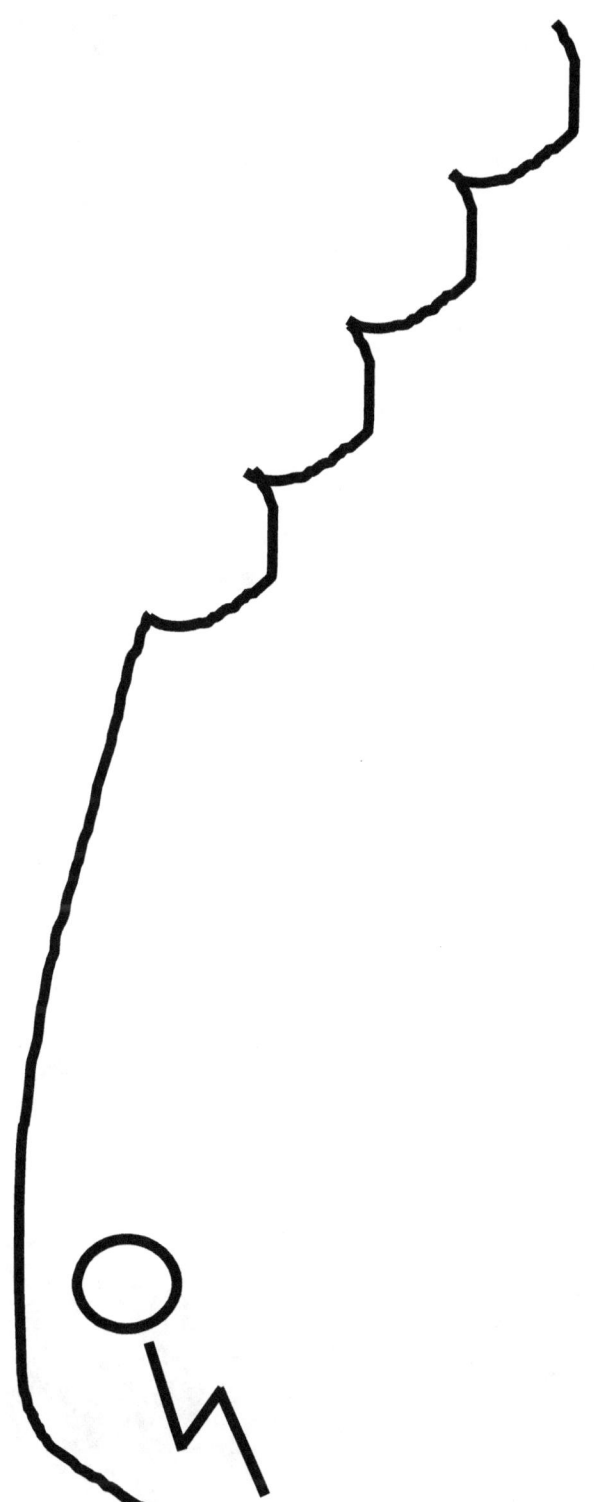

Not Something I Saw

It's not something I saw
On my trip to the West
Although it was going on all the time
Without rest.

Nothing was said
And nothing was seen
But the eyes that all passed
Knew it to be.

It goes on all the time
It's always with us
But the most we seem to do
Is pet it, when it begs us.

For finding meaning
We're at a loss
'Cause the questions people asking
Misplace the force.

Meaning is nothing
Intrinsic to thee
It's just how we group things
It's relations we see.

I saw it all the time
In misguided expression
Confused and abused
Not knowing any better.

Not many of those things
Were seen by these eyes
Except in small bits
Of imaginative play
But it goes on all the time.
All the time, all the time, all the time.

To put one against another
With such shallow symbols
Keeps expression misguided
And always kept hiding.

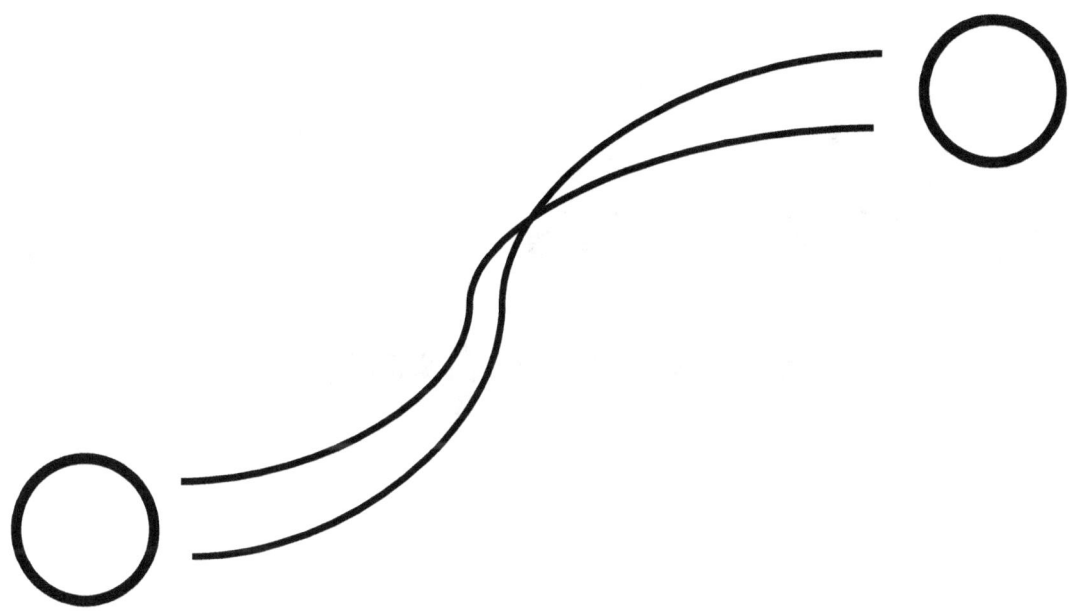

LET **R** = RULES

LET **R** = RELATIONSHIPS

R

33

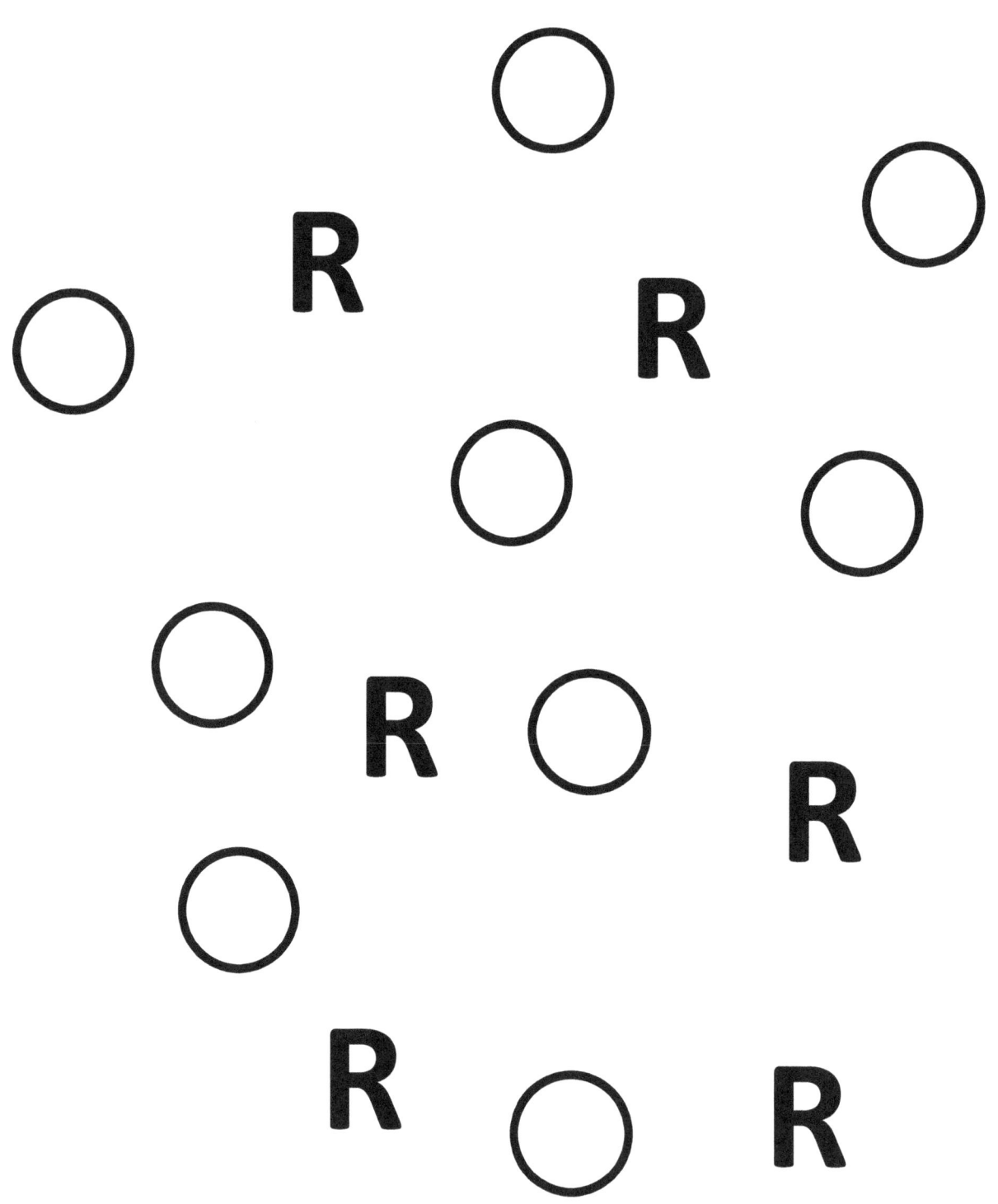

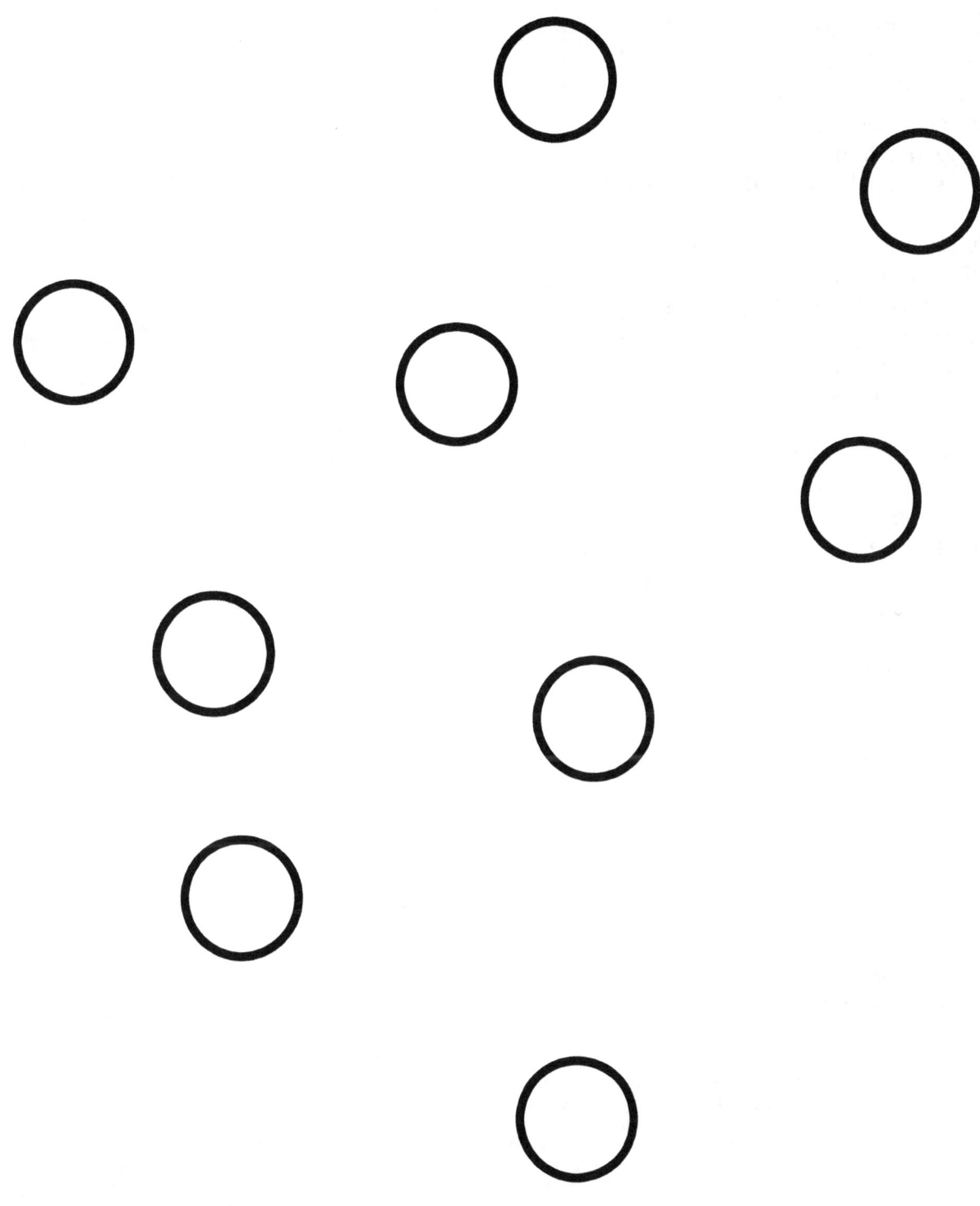

The Establishment

The establishment
Of kinds and classes
That making do require
Some kind of easy,
Recognizable mark
'Cause that what membership desire.

You feel silly
You're not like that
And you want to make amends.
You feel guilty
You don't make it
Inside either end.

But that don't mean
There is no room
It don't mean
You can't be.

It just mean
The world around
Oh, it's just not like
You or me.

Oh, what I see
And what I feel
It's just not
Like that.

And you can't
Tell me
That that's all there is
And all there is is fact.

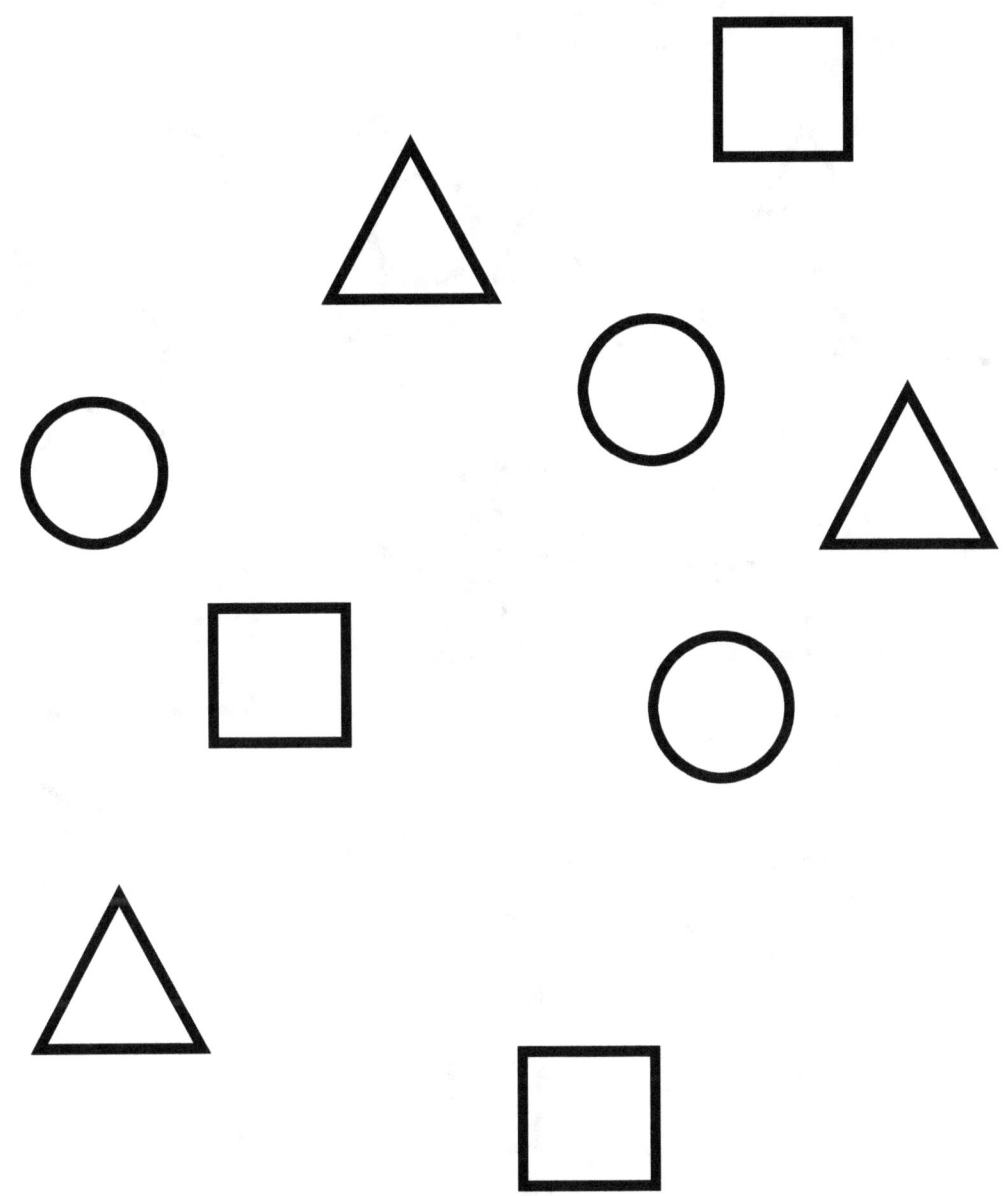

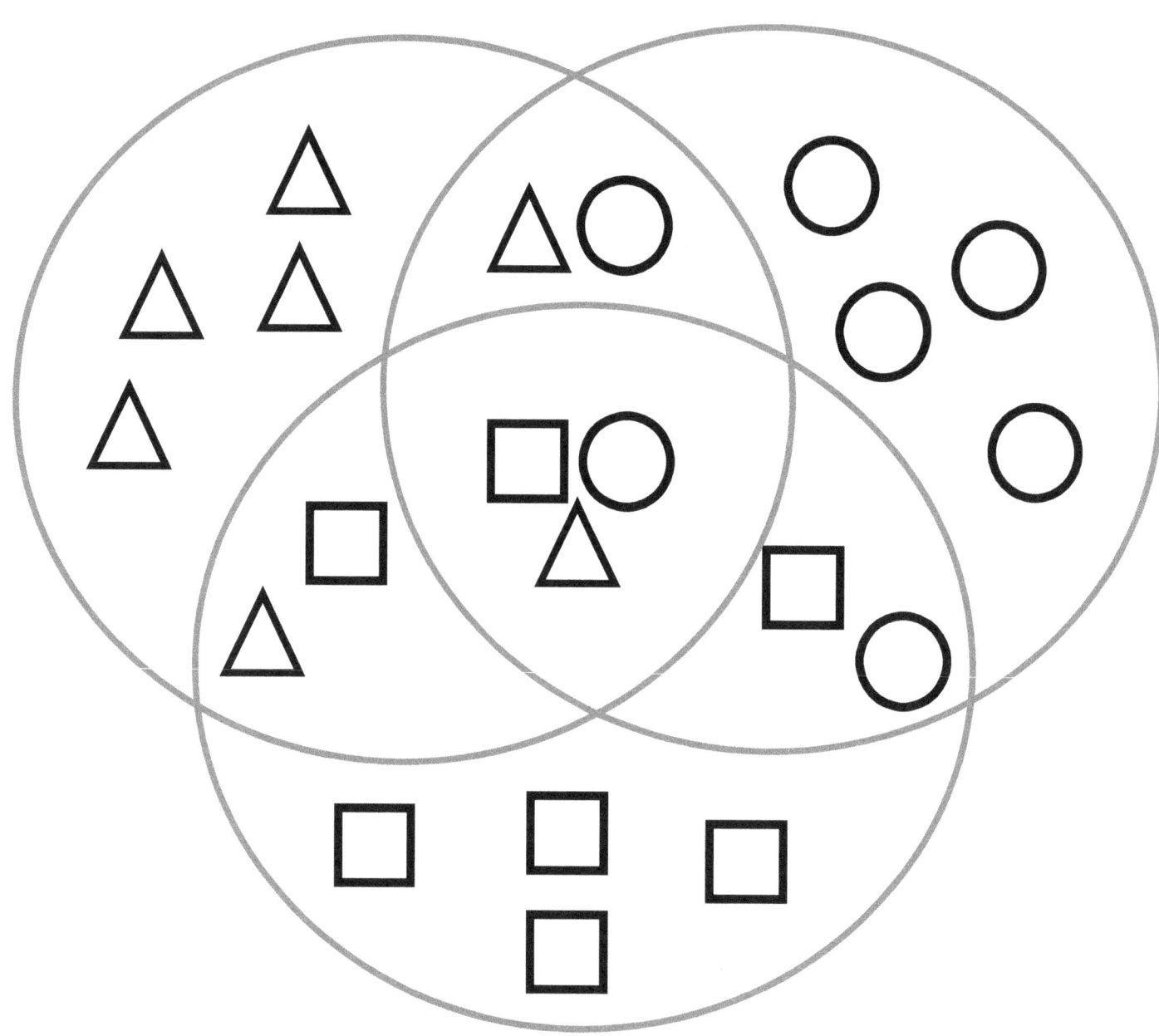

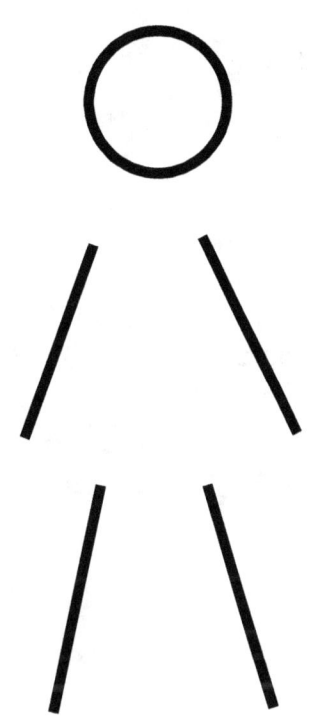

Gliding on a Rainbow

I'm gliding on a rainbow
Down toward heaven on earth
She is a woman
And I've loved her since birth.

I am a man
If you must know
And our children wander near and far
In our happy home.

Life is so pretty here
Sometimes I think I might cry
And whenever I feel the urge coming on
Oh, she's right here by my side.

Happiness comes in all different colors
In all the ways we're related to each other

I'm gliding on a rainbow
Down toward heaven on earth
She is a woman and I'm a man
And we've loved each other since birth.

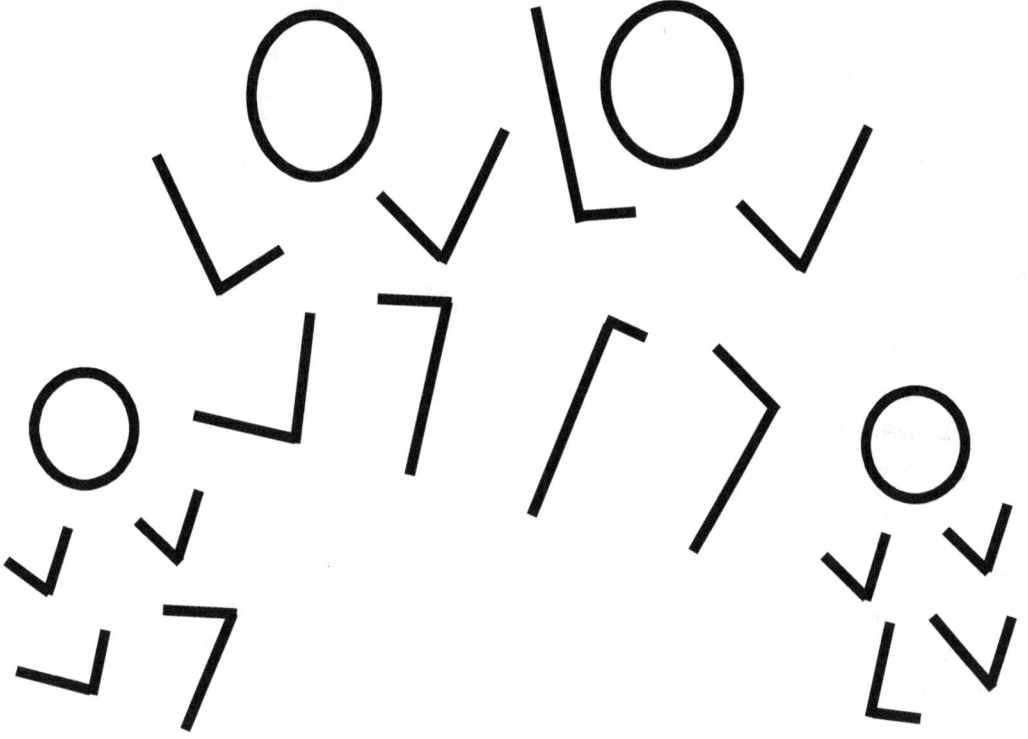

Georgie

Georgie, Georgie
When will you be happy?
Georgie, Georgie
When will you not blame?

Georgie, Georgie
When will you see reality?
Georgie, Georgie
When will you be sane?

I know you just want to
Love the one you're with
I know you just want to
Be loved and forgiven.

Georgie, Georgie
When will you be happy?
I know you just cannot
Feel love or forgive.

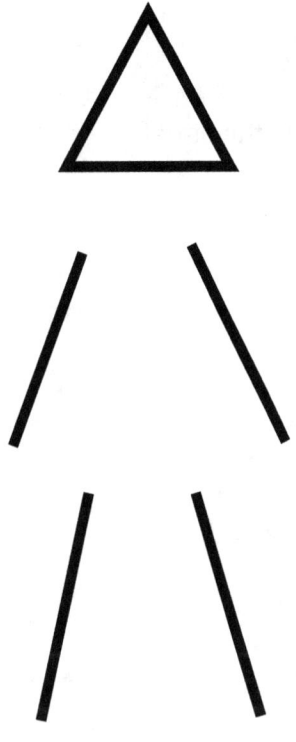

Loyal Disrespect

He's got loyal disrespect for his family
He's got loyal disrespect for his friends
He's got loyal disrespect for his lover
He's got loyal disrespect 'til the end

He's got loyal disrespect for his brother
He's got loyal disrespect for his son
He's got loyal disrespect for his man in the street
He's so lousy he won't respect no one.

Now he sits there thinks he's so charming
Sits there acting so cool
Sits there feels he's so graceful
But he sit and break all the rules

Now the man seem to hide his feeling
So that nothing seem to make much sense
He'll smile when he thinking you ugly
And he'll laugh when he wish you was dead.

She's got loyal disrespect for her family
She's got loyal disrespect for her friends
She's got loyal disrespect for her lover
She's got loyal disrespect 'til the end

She's got loyal disrespect for her brother
She's got loyal disrespect for her son
She's got loyal disrespect for his woman in the street
She's so lousy she won't respect no one.

Now she sits there thinks she's so charming
Sits there acting so cool
Sits there feels she's so graceful
But she sit and break all the rules

Now the woman seem to hide her feeling
So that nothing seem to make much sense
She'll smile when she thinking you ugly
And she'll laugh when she wish you was dead.

Loyal disrespect.

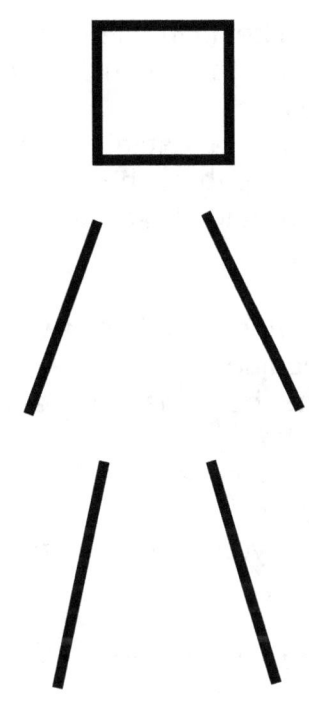

Her Sweet Shoulder

I cried on her sweet
shoulder
She held me close to
her
I knew not what I did
But said: Take me as I
am.

I cried on her sweet
shoulder
She held me tight and
warm
A glimpse of feeling
naked
Will you take me as I
am?

She held me close
against her
Cradled in her hands
She knew not what she
did
But said: I love you as
you stand.

I cried on her sweet
shoulder
She held me close to
her
I knew not what I did
But said: Take me as I
am.

I love to be the best to
her
I thought that is what love
did mean
Being what she needs
Is all I meant to be.

And being true to myself
I thought I could have
both
Then a spirit came
surging through
And said: Take me as I
am.

I cried on her sweet
shoulder
She held me tight and
warm
A glimpse of feeling
naked
Will you take me as I
am?

She held me close
against her
Cradled in her hands
She knew not what she
did
But said: I love you as
you stand.

I cried on her sweet
shoulder
I want her oh so bad
You are the only one who
knows me deep
You are the only one I
have

There are some things
only time will give
Given two spirits that
flow free
To meet and greet and
want each other
Two spirits, you and me.

I cried on her sweet
shoulder
She held me close to her
I knew not what I did
But said: Take me as I
am.

I cried on her sweet
shoulder
I knew not what I did
But said take me as I am
Sweet Love
And that's just what Love
did give.

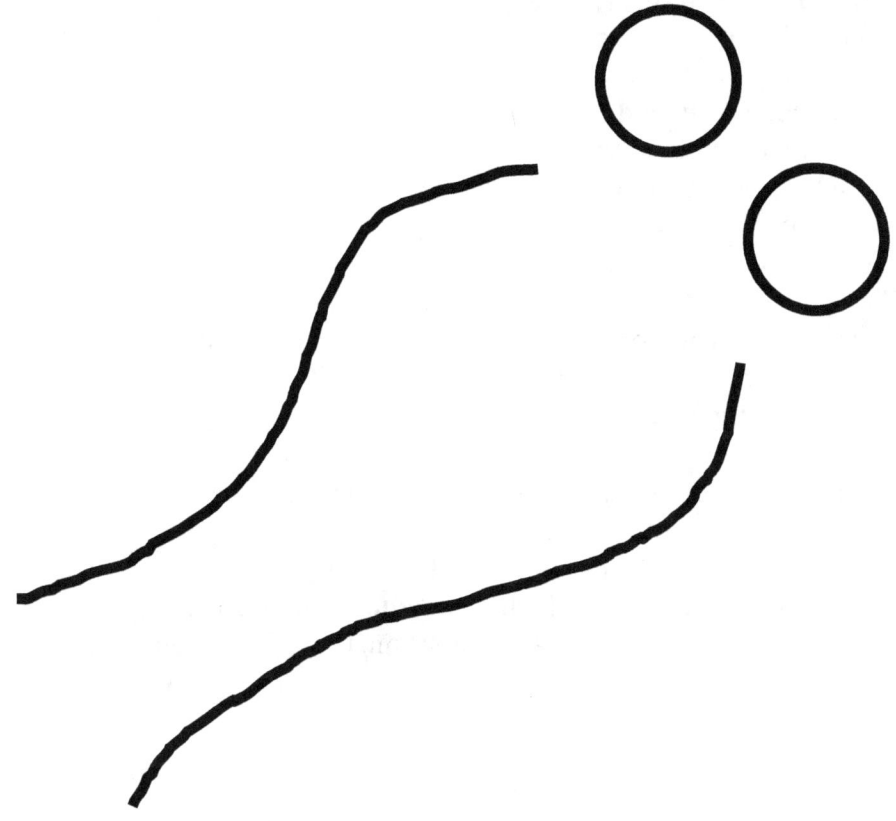

LANGUAGE

When words fail us, we can resort to pictures.
When pictures fail us, we can resort to language.
Not to words alone, but to language.
Language is a structure we create
by forming relationships between words.
In so doing, we create mental pictures of our thoughts.
In song we set those thoughts to music.
Songs in the key of see.

PROPOSITIONS

A proposition is the expression of a relationship between elements.
A proposition can be expressed in words.
Or in forms other than language.

A proposition can have a truth value. It can be true or false.
A proposition can be meaningful. Or meaningless.
A proposition can express something that is real. Or fake.
A proposition can have a truth value which is known. Or unknown.
If there is confusion about the status of a proposition, there is conceptual confusion.

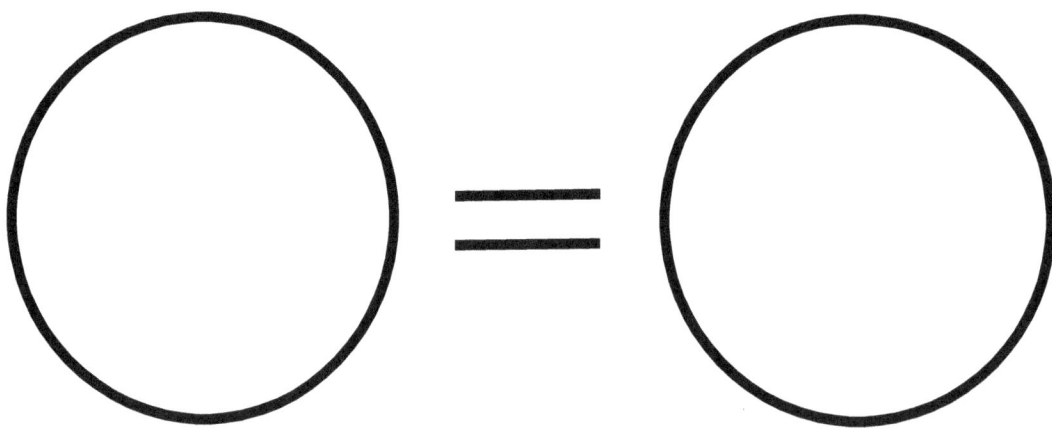

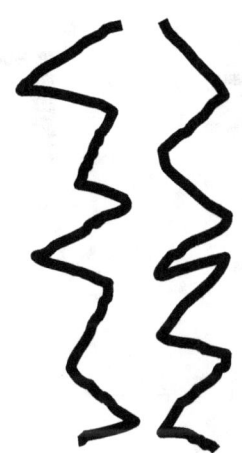

= **DNA**

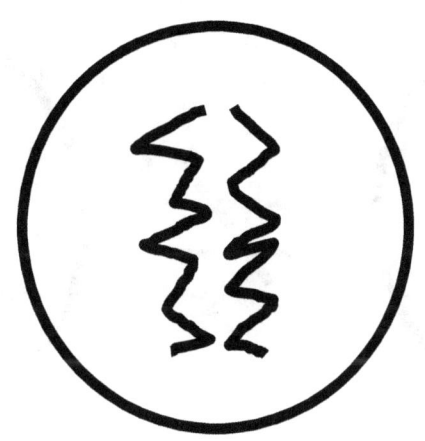

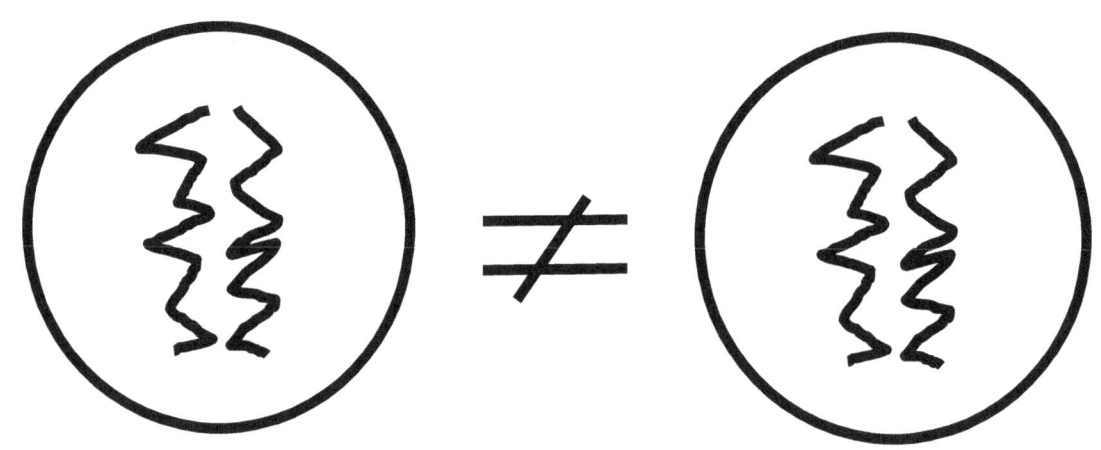

QUESTIONS

A question is an ambiguous proposition. Its answer determines its meaning.

What is the primary unit of activity in human society?

If our answer is that the *primary unit of activity* in human society is the *individual*, a unique human being, then the structure of human society takes on specific *attributes* and *qualities* which arise from this answer and *this* concept.

If we answer that the *primary unit of activity* in human society is the *group*, and human society is composed of distinct groups of human beings, then the structure of human society takes on specific *attributes* and *qualities* which arise from that answer and *that* concept.

This and that.

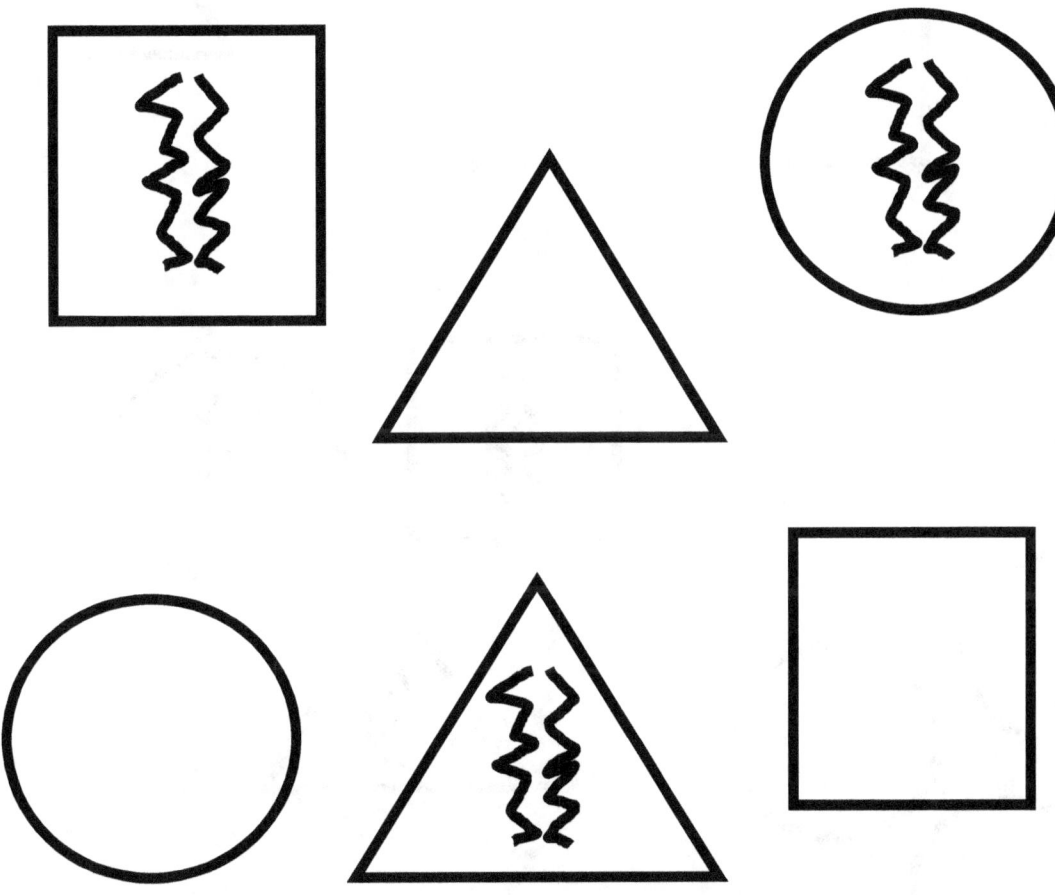

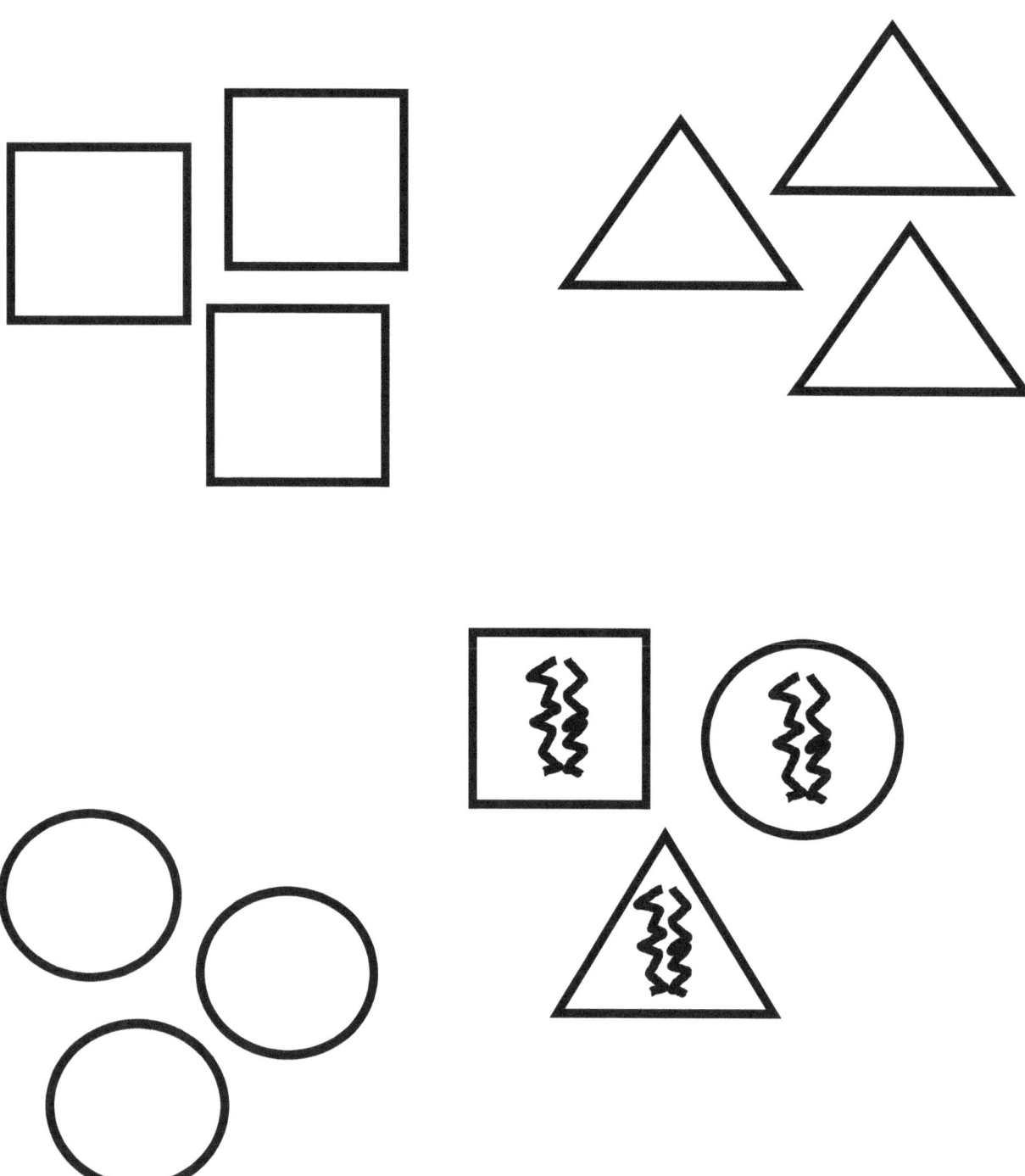

DISTINCT CONCEPTS

Is the primary unit of activity in human society the individual or the group? The answer shapes our ideas about the structure of human society and determines its attributes and qualities. These attributes and qualities, and the concepts that follow from them, need not be the same.

In fact, they likely are not the same.

They may share some features, but the *social structures* arising from two different answers to the same question *are by no means identical.*

And so our ideas about social reality arise from the very nature of our questions about social organization and structure. And from our answers to those questions.

Not all human societies are the same just because the elements which compose them are human beings who we want to think about as equal.

KEY QUESTIONS

What are the most important questions to be asked about the social life of human beings?

Do we see society as composed *primarily* of individual human beings?

Or is human society composed *primarily* of groups of human beings?

Is "to thine own self be true" true?

And what are the rules which bind human beings together as elements in a social network?

What does the structure of human society look like if the *primary unit of activity* is taken to be the *individual*?

What does the structure of human society look like if the *primary unit of activity* is taken to be the *group*?

What is the structure of a social organization if we establish *rules* that promote the equality and freedom of *unique individual* human beings?

What is the structure of a social organization if we establish *rules* that promote the equality and freedom of *unique groups* of individual human beings?

What are the relationships between the elements which we take as the primary unit of activity in the social organization of human beings? How are these relationships defined and expressed?

What is the relationship between the individual and the group?

How can we make unique individual human beings equal to each other? Is that question an oxymoron?

How can we make one group of individual human beings, who are members of the group because they share one or more distinct and defining characteristics, equal to other groups which share a different set of defining characteristics? Another oxymoron?

And what happens when unique groups of individuals intermingle and give rise to individuals who do not fit the form of any existing group?

What do we mean by diversity as an attribute of a group of people each of whom exists as a unique human being? Is that organization made more diverse by dividing it into distinct groups of individuals?

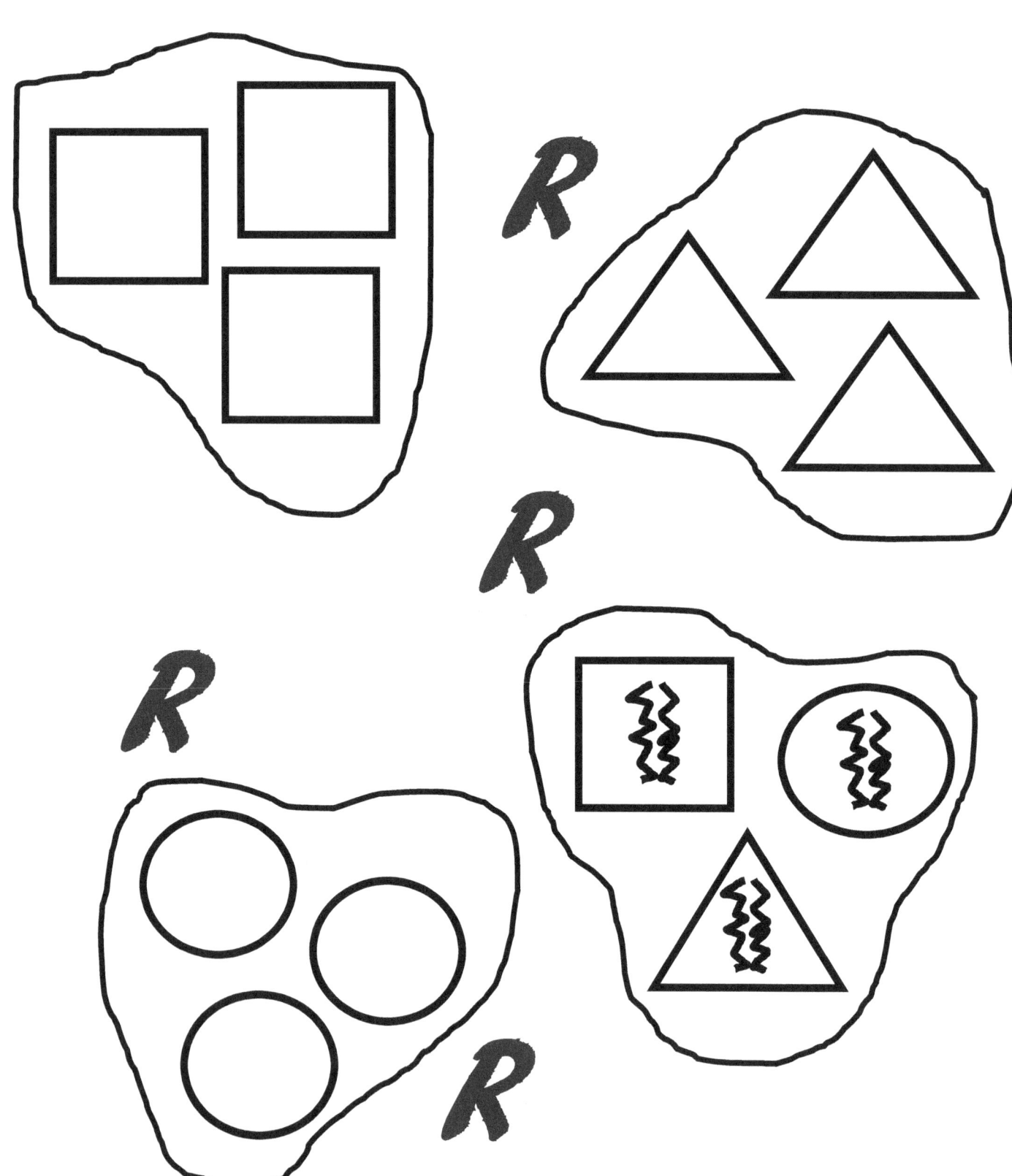

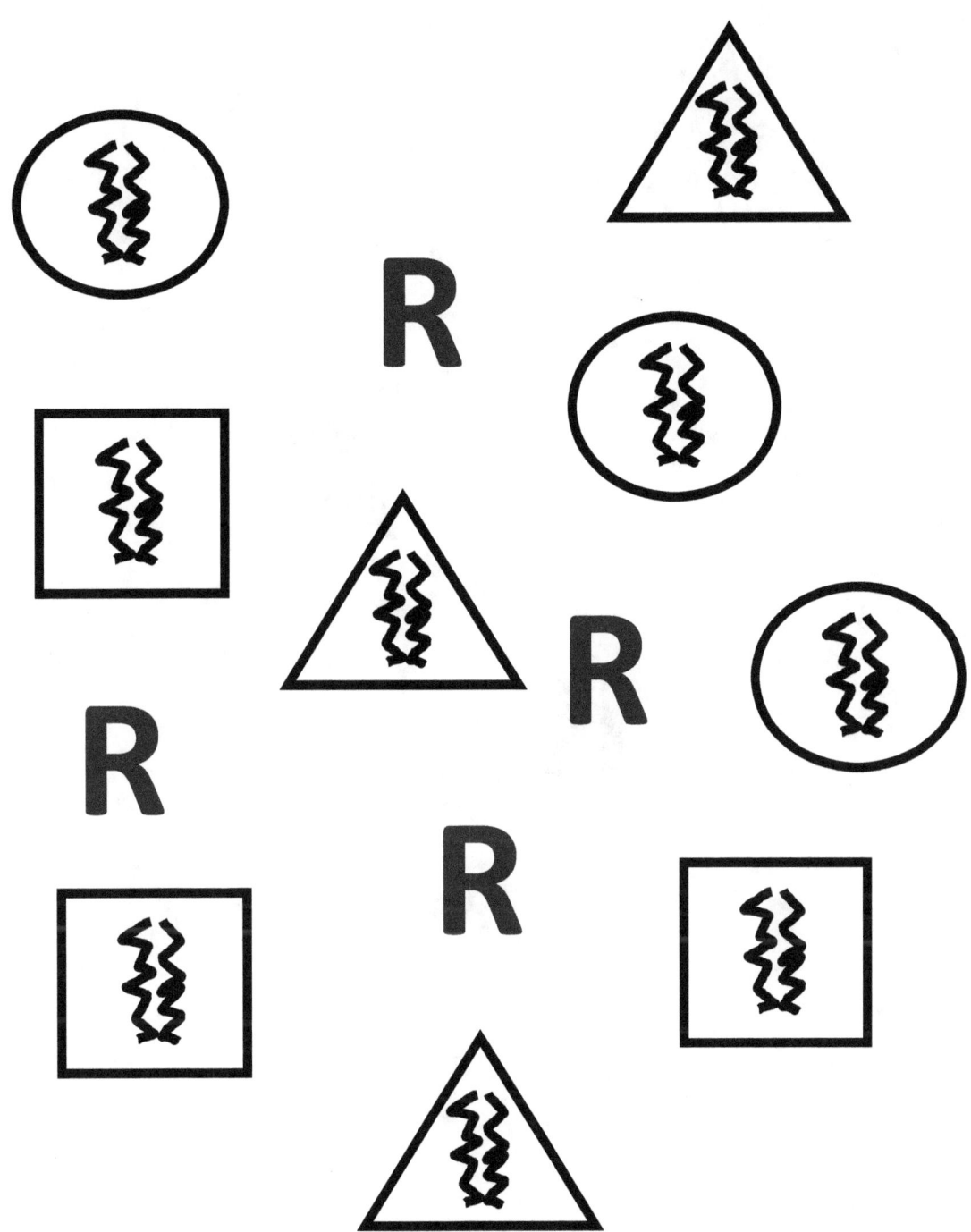

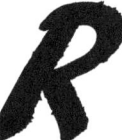

R

R

PARADOX

Paradox is a sign of conceptual confusion.

Paradox creates conceptual tension. That tension is released when a conceptual context is developed that resolves the conceptual confusion.

To resolve these paradoxical concepts, human beings must explore the meaning of equality and freedom in the context of these kinds of questions. We must explore the meaning of diversity.

Are the rules that make unique *individuals* free and equal in human society different than the rules that make distinct *groups* composed of unique, individual human beings free and equal? And, if these are different sets of rules, is there any way to integrate them in the same set of rules?

How does one go about *maintaining* the social reality of individual liberty and freedom?

Suppose that, after a period of due diligence, hard work, and hard-won battles, a set of rules is established and put into play which promotes *individual* equality and liberty. What happens if, after these rules are created and put into play, as reality, a faction, a group of individuals, forms and that group argues that the *rules and relationships* which protect the equality and freedom of each unique individual, rules which exist as the defining culture and the basis of social reality in a nation-state, *are not constant but variable*, that they are instead living and breathing, subject to change, constant, never-ending change, and may evolve in any which way they may?

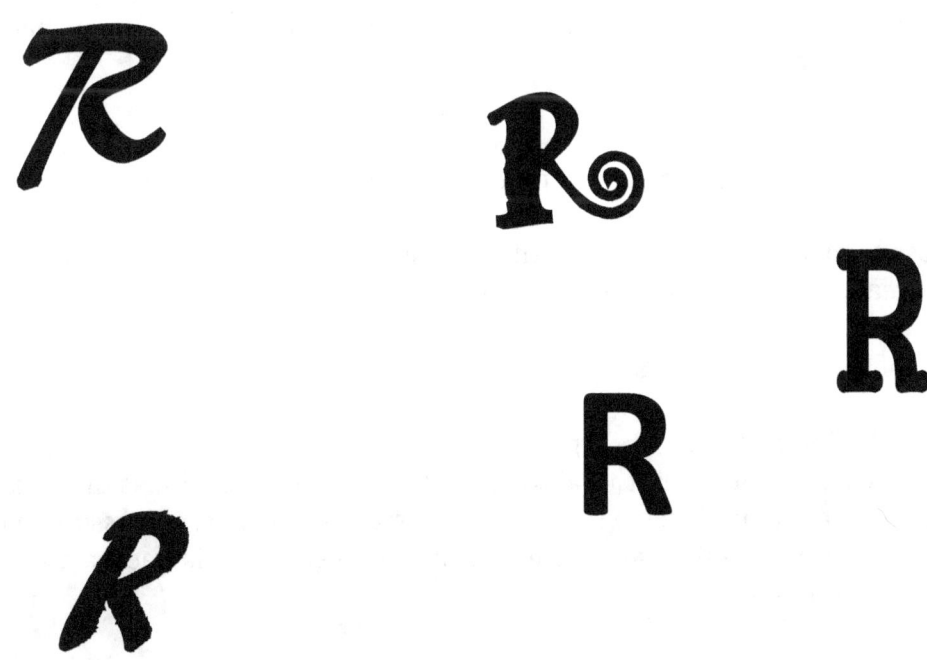

SOCIAL SYSTEMS

How are the interests of unique individuals best integrated into a social system? How are the interests of groups of individuals best integrated?

What is power in society? How is it created? How is it distributed? How is it transferred?

What is value in society? How is it created? How is it distributed? How is it transferred?

And how are these things destroyed?

How do distinct social systems integrate as a society and as a nation?

How do different nation-states function together?

What happens to human beings roaming the Earth as morality, the constellation of rules that guide human behavior, evolves and de-evolves, twists and turns, stabilizes and then destabilizes, comes and goes, over time?

Is there a unifying vision of human society that is noble and worth fighting for? Fighting to keep?

Is there a social reality that functions as a stabilizing force for human beings given the gift of life on this one and only Earth?

PROPAGANDA

Propaganda is the intentional communication of false ideas under the pretense of truth and honesty.

Not all individuals who make false statements are liars. Some just might not see the truth or grasp reality.

The most effective propaganda imbues the ideas it seeks to express and propagate with feeling, often intense feeling, making it more difficult for an individual human being to process the information objectively.

LOGIC AND REALITY

Applying principles of logic to perceptions of reality creates *potential* facts. Individuals who engage in such activity are logicrats. Those who do not are illogicrats.

Logicrats who test their concepts against reality classify those concepts that are wholly analogous to how reality is observed to behave as *facts*. True concepts.

Such is the nature of scientific thinking.

How is the social reality of human beings living together impacted when a group of individuals ignore facts and choose not to allow facts to influence their ideas or behavior? And what happens when potential facts are adopted as established facts, and assumed to be true, even though there is uncertainty as to whether or not these potential facts actually are true when tested against reality?

All concepts have a logical form. An analogy exists when two different ideas or concepts share the same logical form.

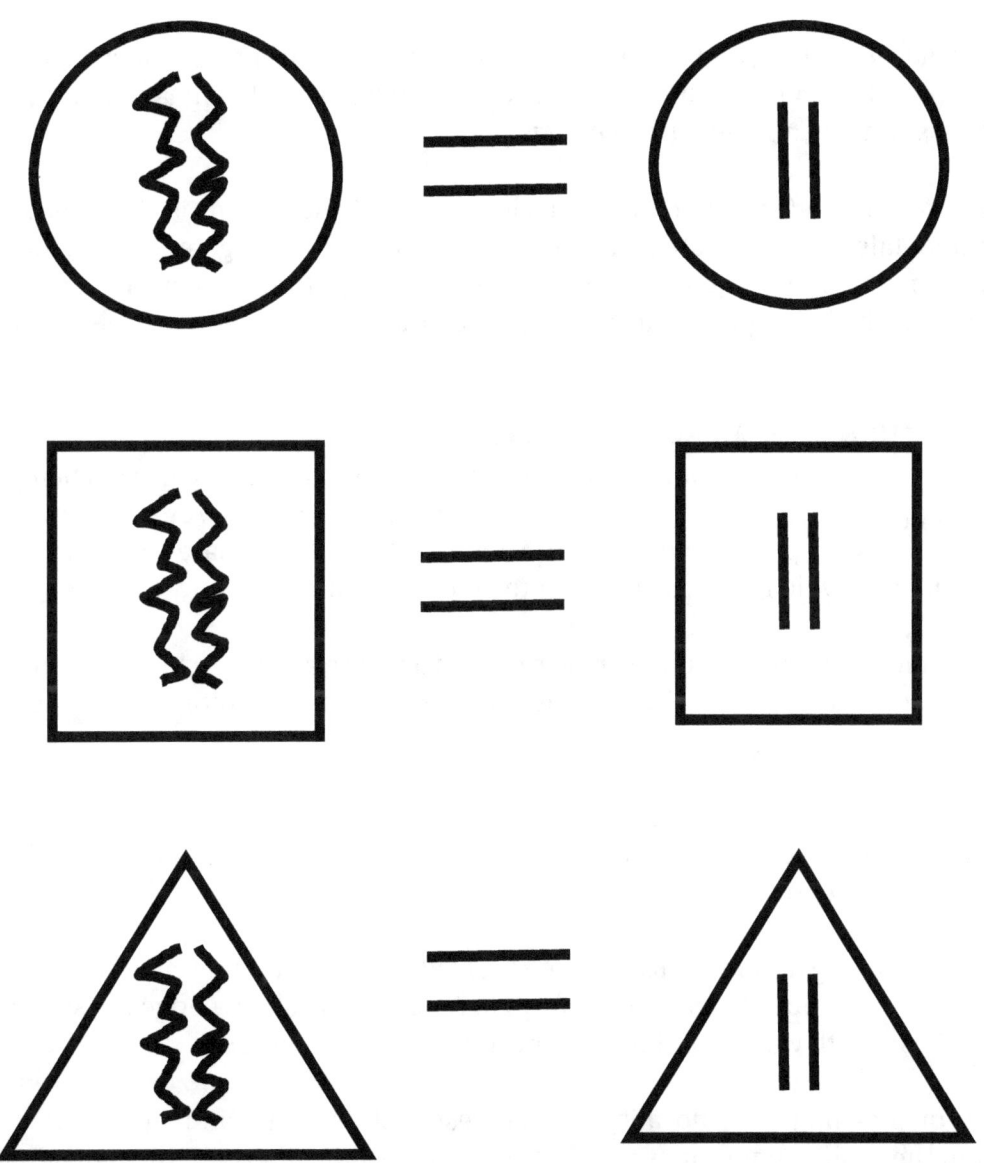

POORLY DIFFERENTIATED CONCEPTS

When thought is composed of a potpourri of concepts of various truth values, and analogies are created using concepts with similar but not exactly congruent and perhaps predominantly discordant logical forms, thinking becomes guided by ideas the truth value of which is difficult to determine. These poorly differentiated concepts can lead the human mind to postulate causal relationships which are assumed to be true even though they are not; or their truth value is uncertain.

Thought which is promulgated using poorly differentiated concepts, or concepts whose truth value is incorrectly labelled, can create conceptual malignancy. Malignant concepts destroy the fabric of social life among human beings.

Malignant concepts often originate from ideas whose logical form is ill-defined, or ideas which contain false or inaccurate analogies, and which are promulgated as true nonetheless. Malignant thought arises when concepts of this kind are put forth as established fact, when they should be labelled as potential facts or propositions the truth valve of which is unknown or uncertain.

THE RESURRECTION OF MEANING AND MORALITY

Our crisis of meaning and morality can be resolved as more and more human beings develop an appreciation of the significance of *words, language, pictures, relationships, and rules* in creating concepts grounded in *truth* and *reality*; and articulate such concepts for all to understand and which, in turn, are used to guide human activity.

Our crisis of meaning and morality can be resolved as more and more human beings become skilled in the perception of reality and the creation of understanding by the application of logic.

Our crisis of meaning and morality can be resolved as more and more human beings embrace ideas derived from observation; ideas which have been tried and tested; ideas which history teaches *fit the form of reality*.

Our crisis of meaning and morality can be resolved as more and more human beings reject ideas which history shows do *not* fit the form of reality; and acknowledge the status of those concepts whose truth value is unknown, uncertain, or meaningless.

Our crisis of meaning and morality can be resolved as more and more human beings understand the fundamental rules and facts that protect the liberty of the individual human being; and create a social structure that *promotes the equality of unique human beings living together as individuals*; individuals who may be seen as belonging to different groups and living together in families, in villages, in towns, in cities, in States, and in Nations.

The numerous Nations which cover the face of the Earth are, in fact, entities composed of individual human beings who exist in the context of meaning and morality, and these primary living units function together to constitute the social life of human beings.

These songs celebrate individuality, love, spirit, family, and community. And life on Earth.

These songs celebrate meaning and morality.

Songs in the Key of See.

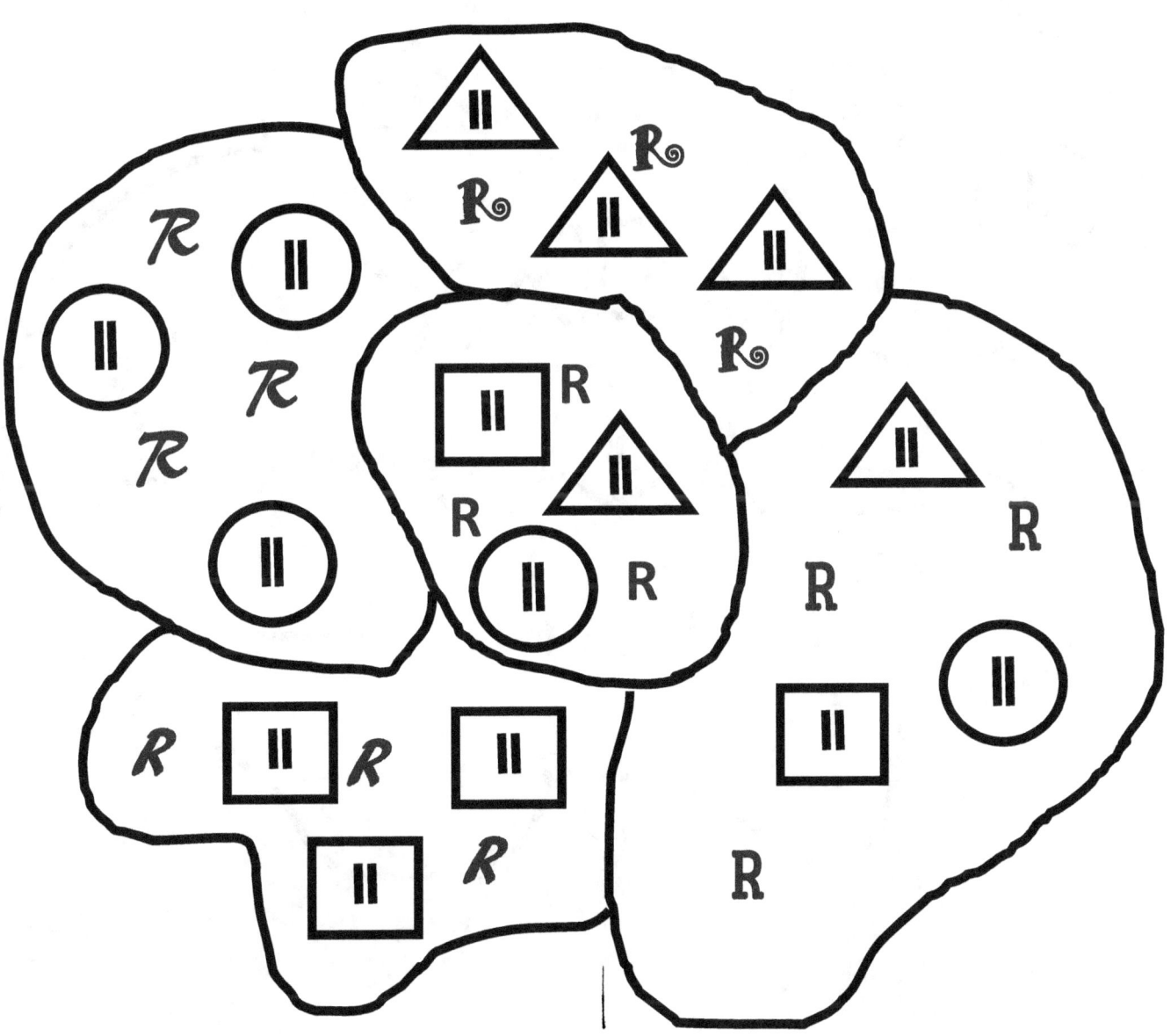

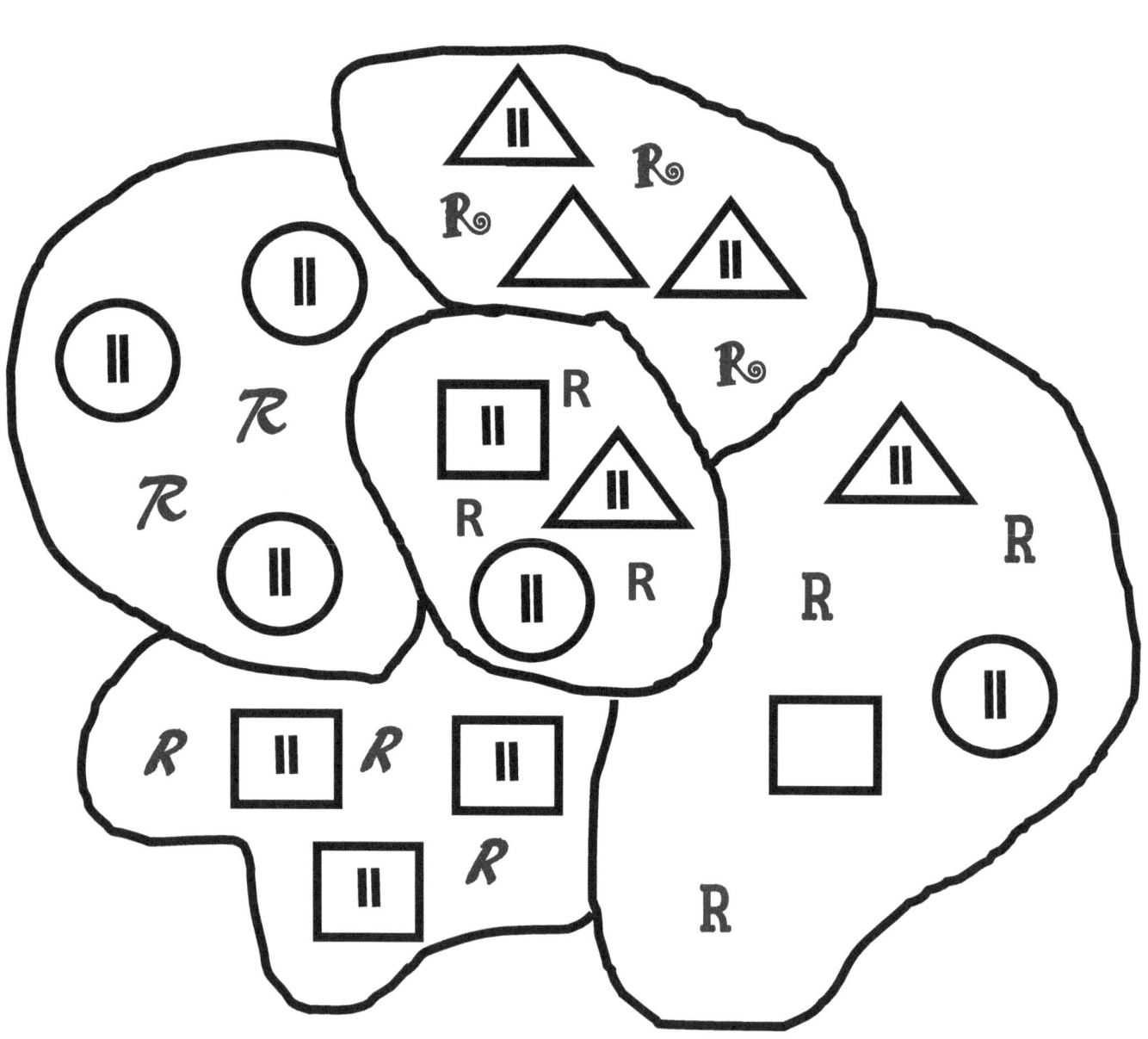

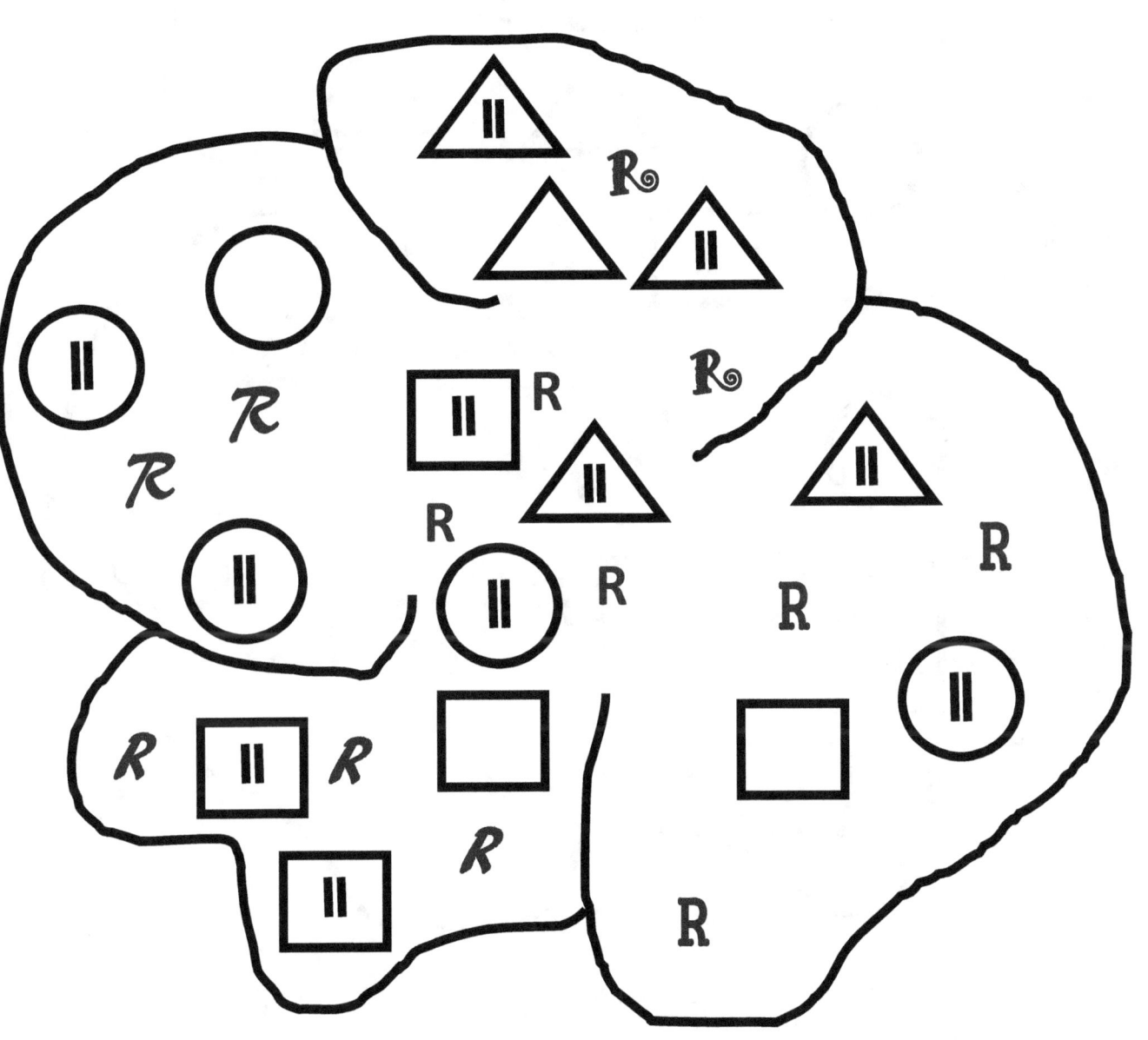

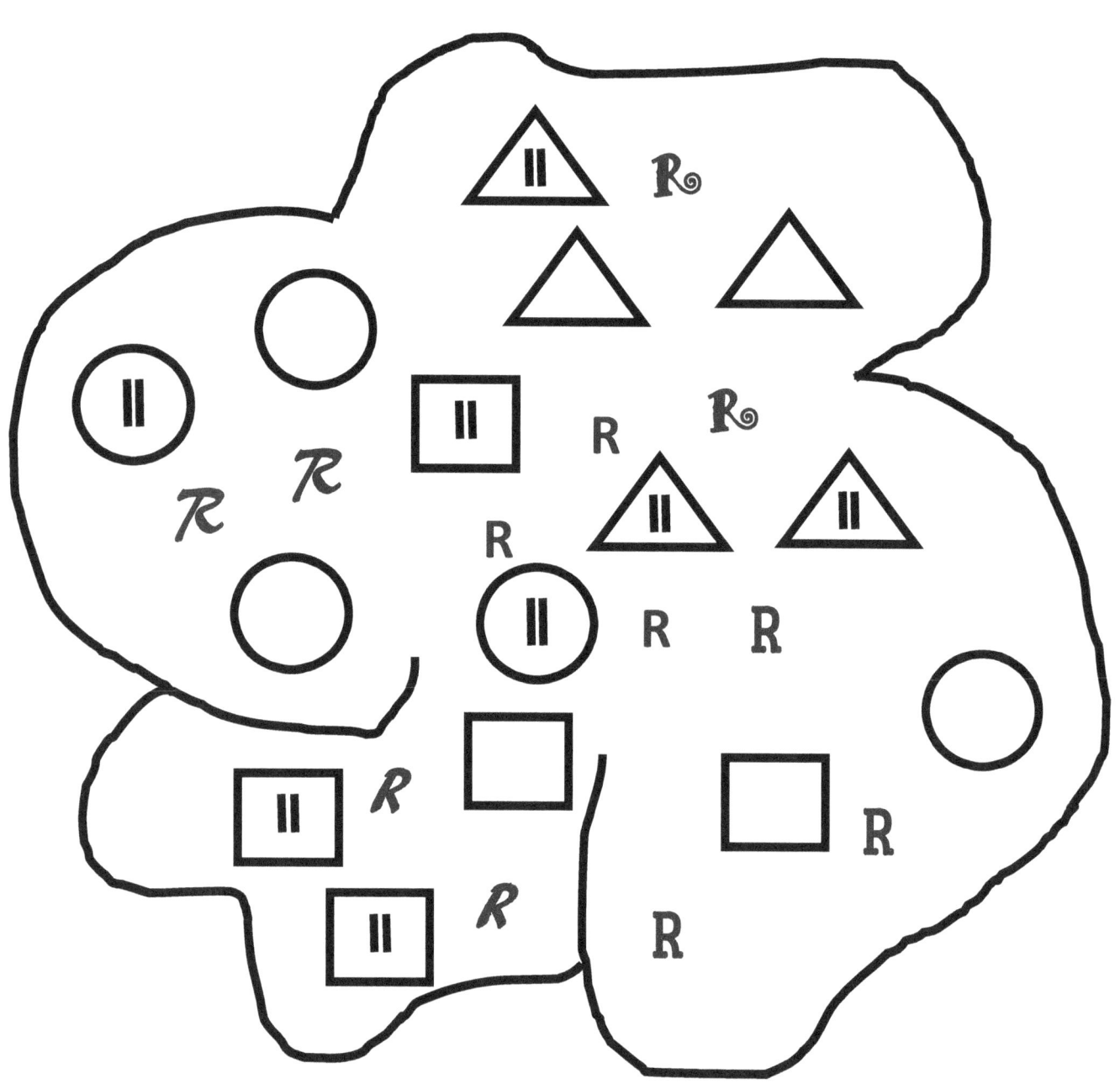

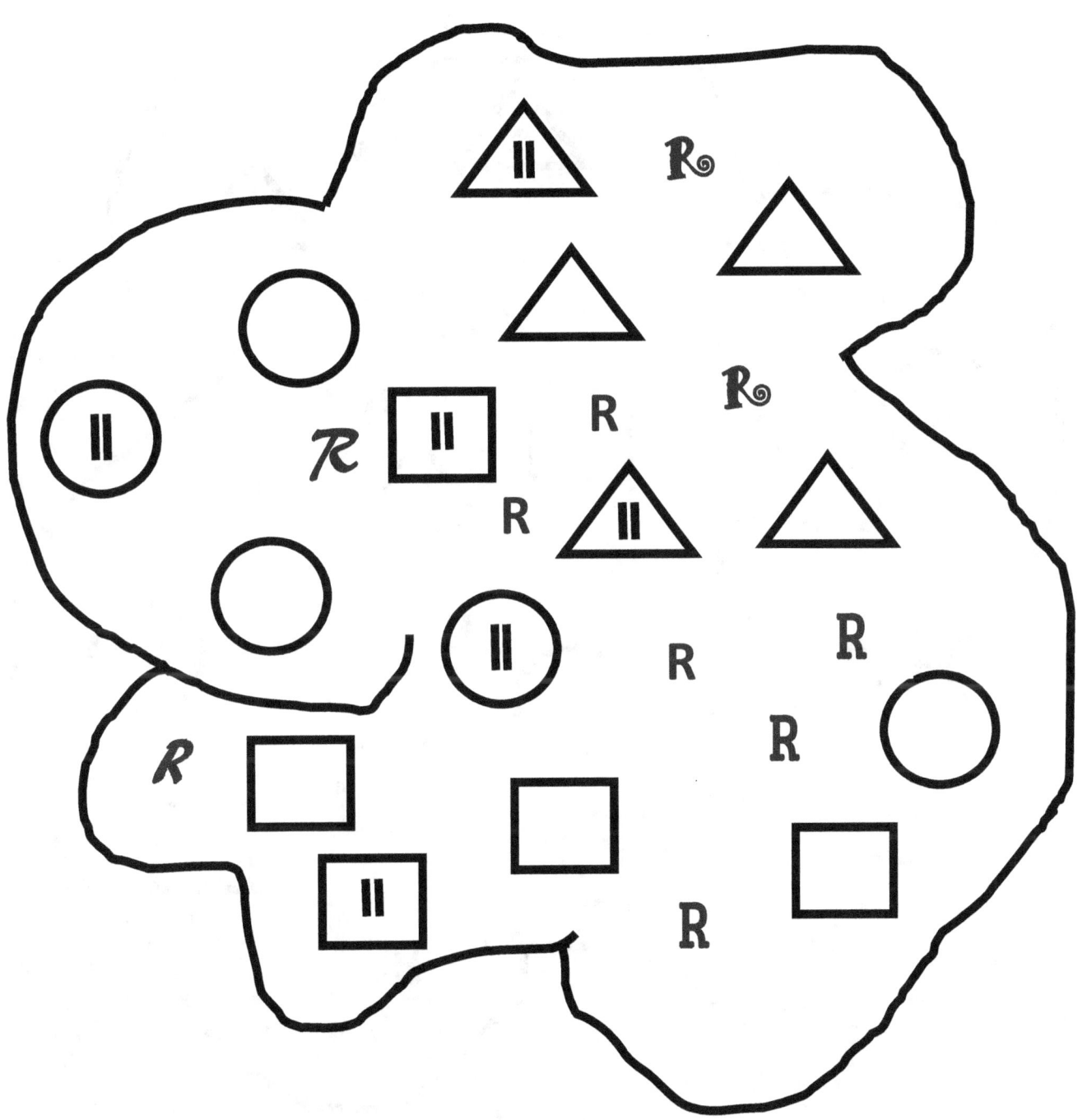

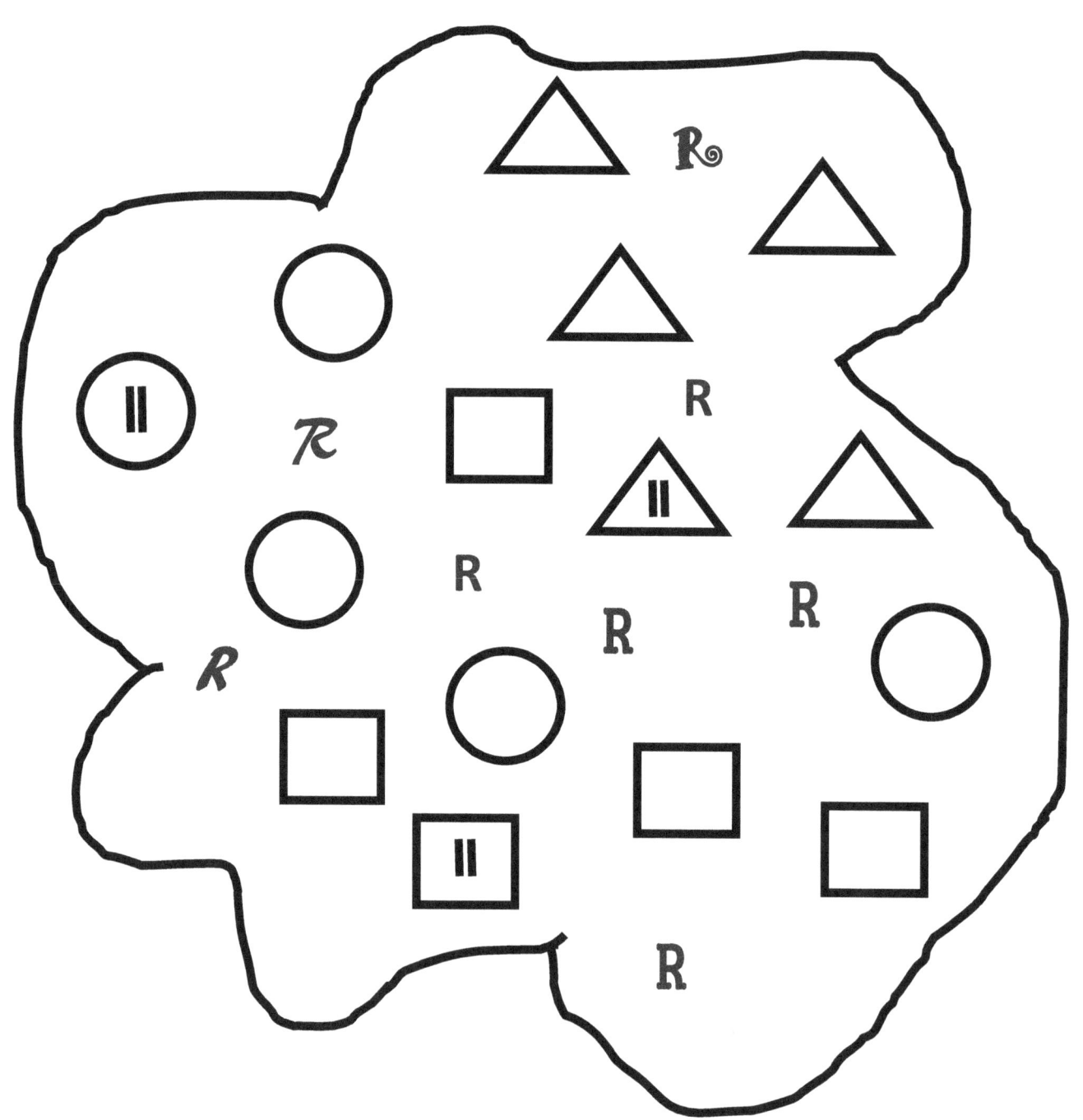

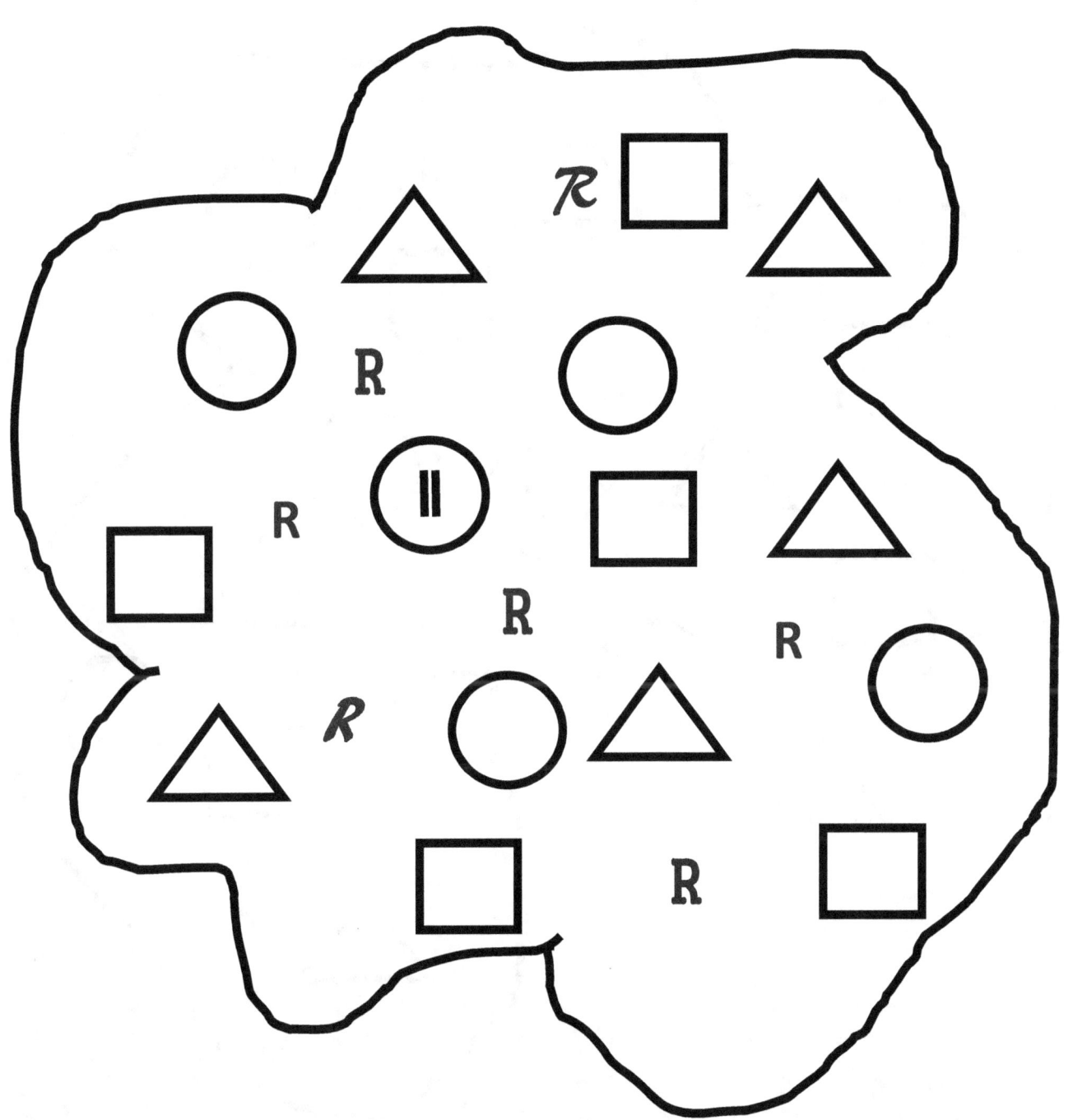

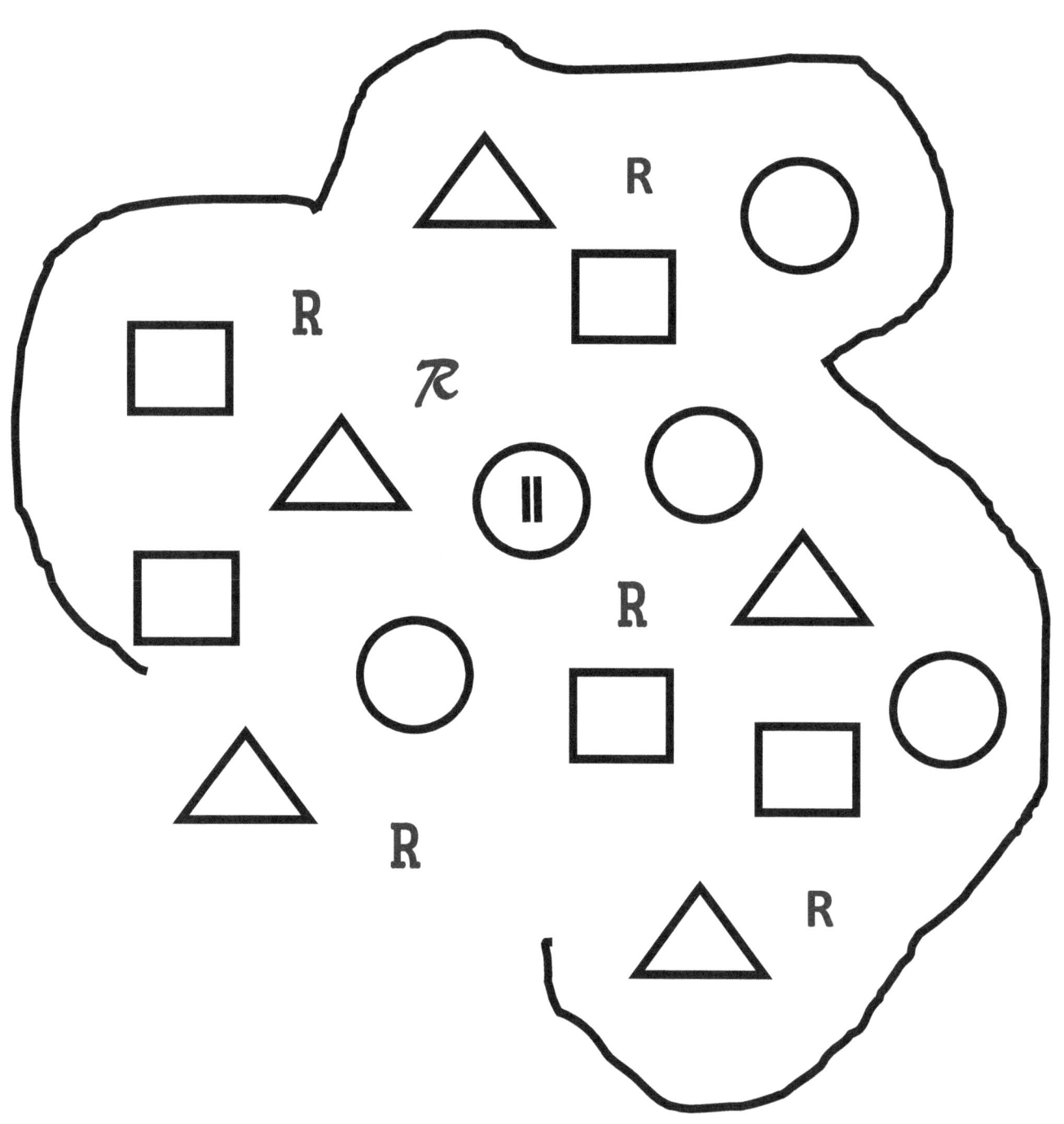

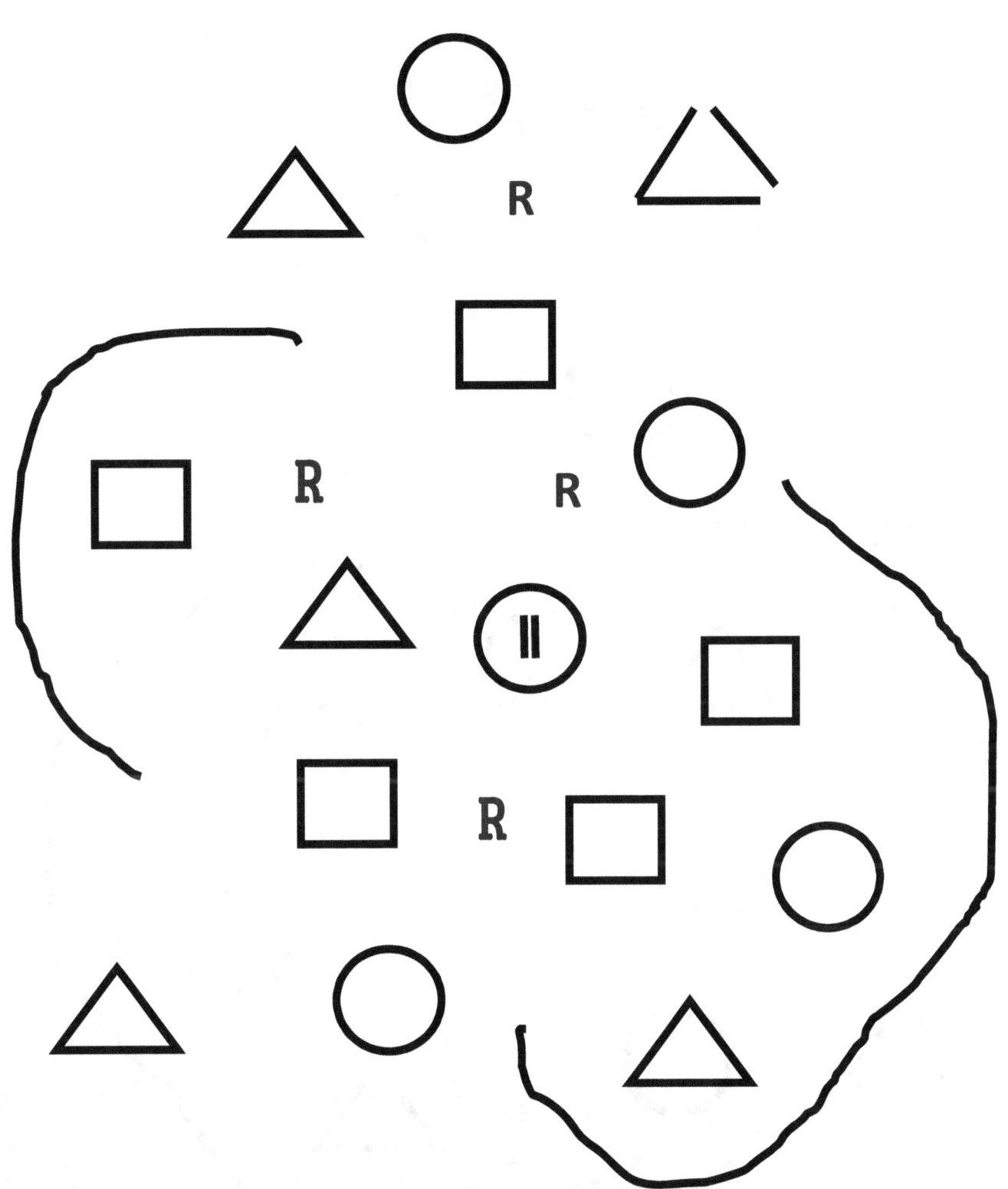

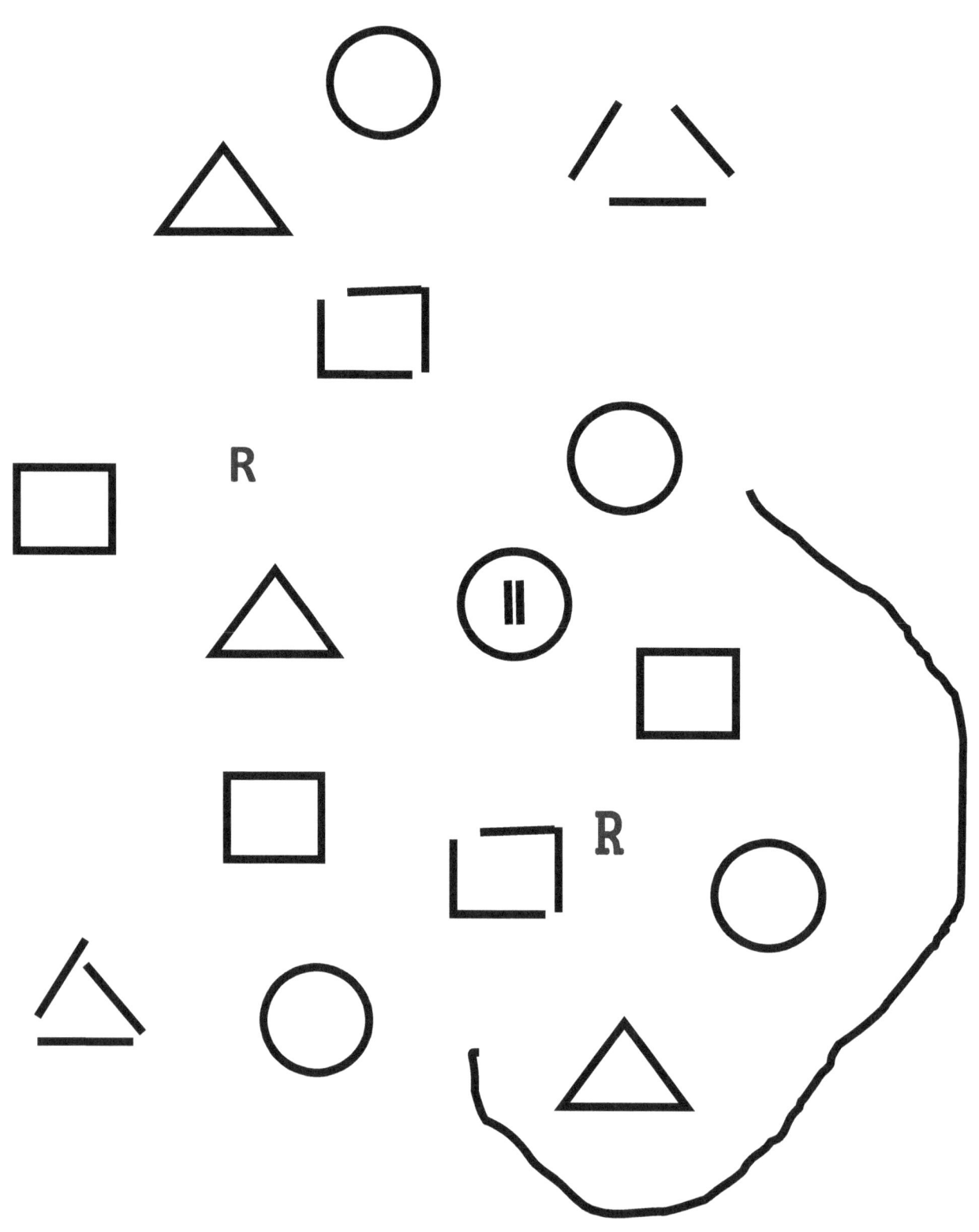

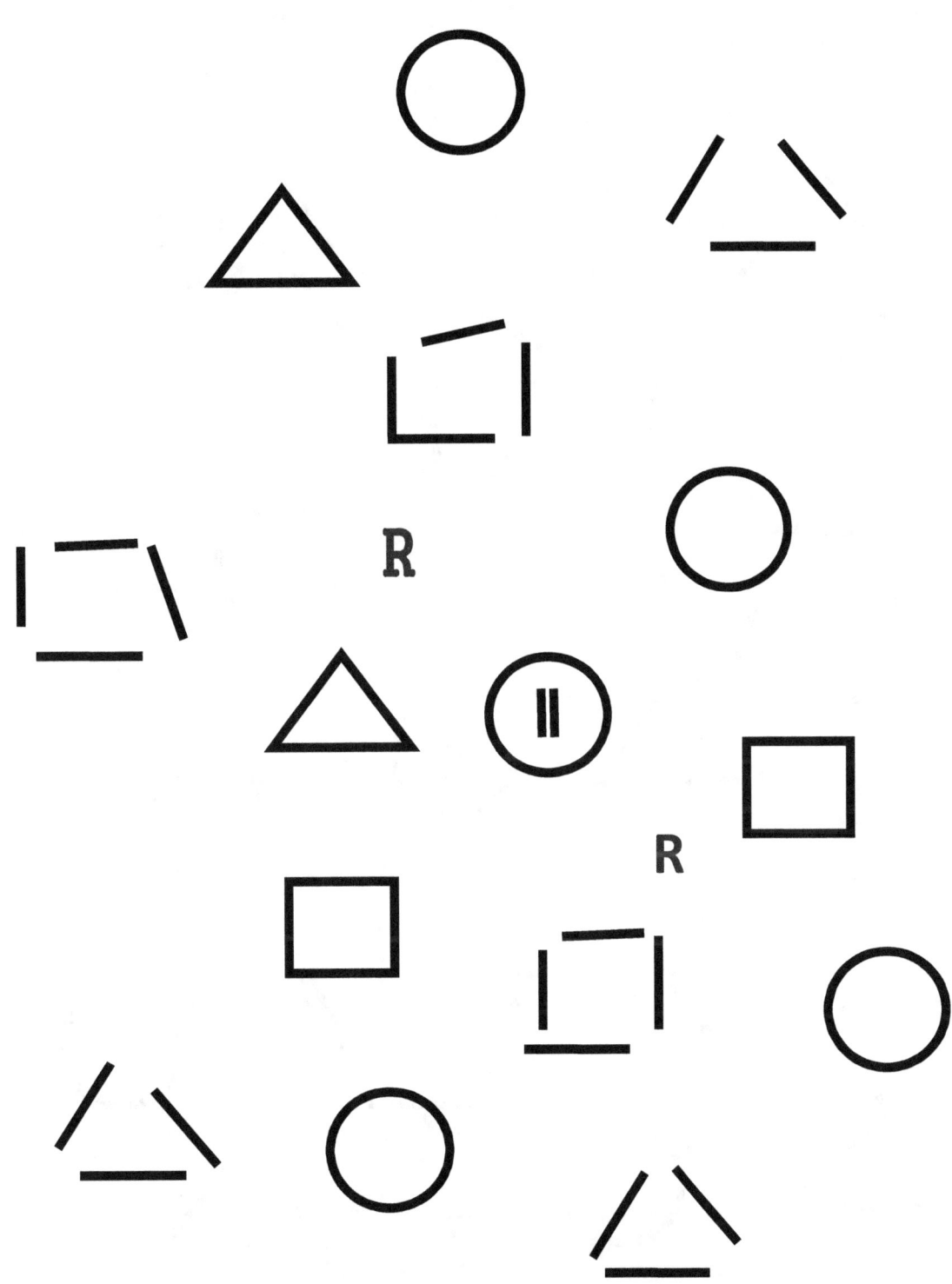

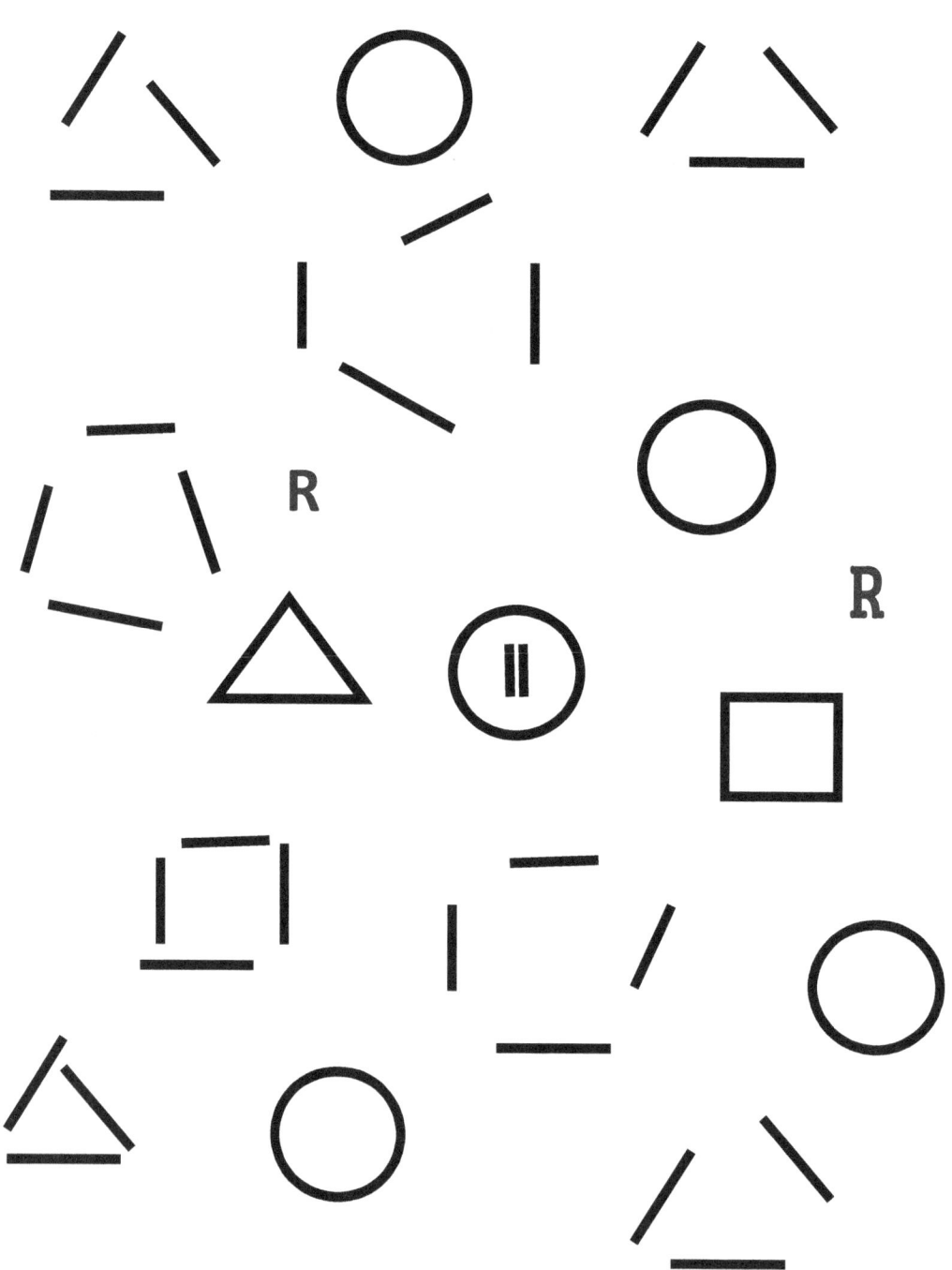

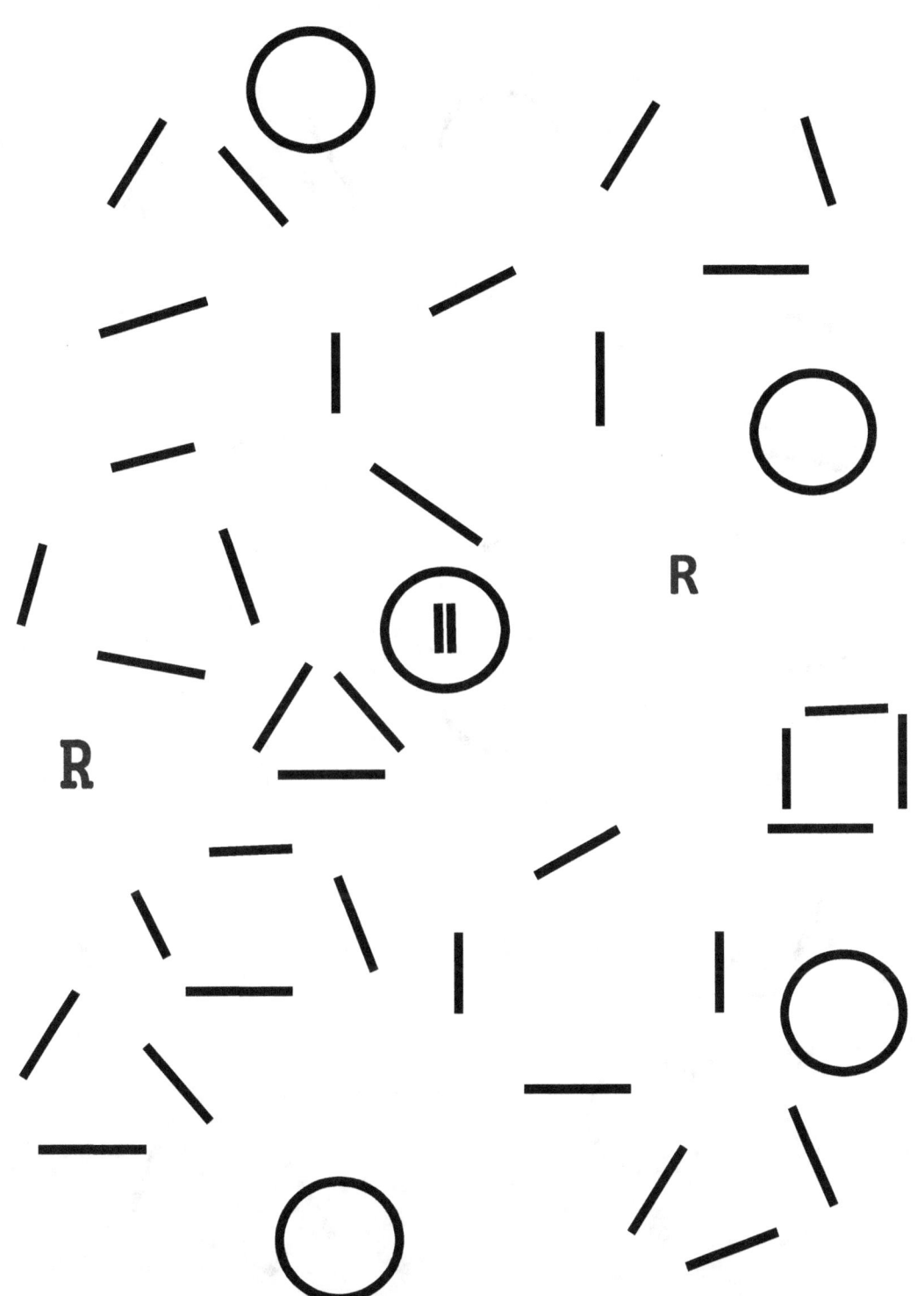

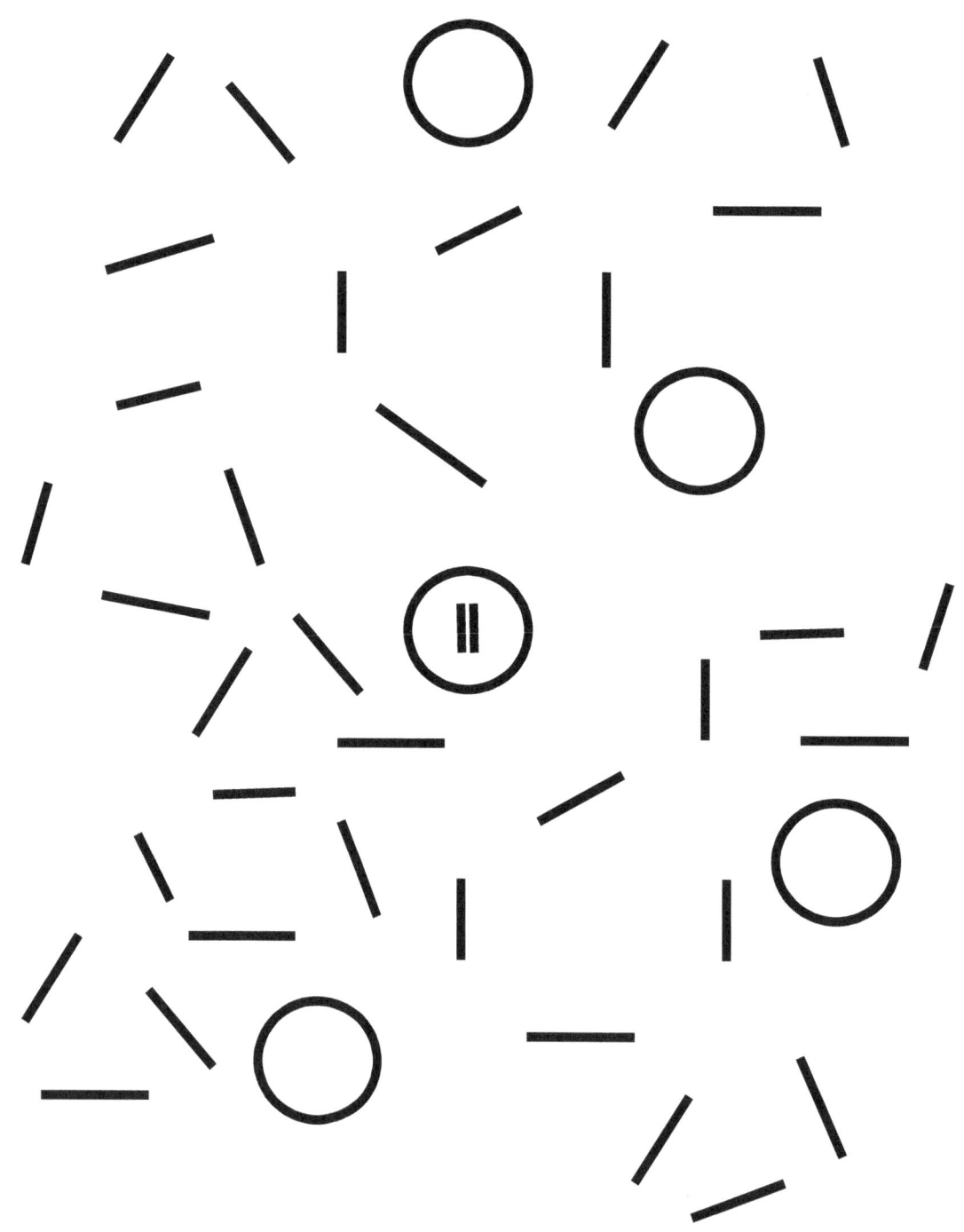

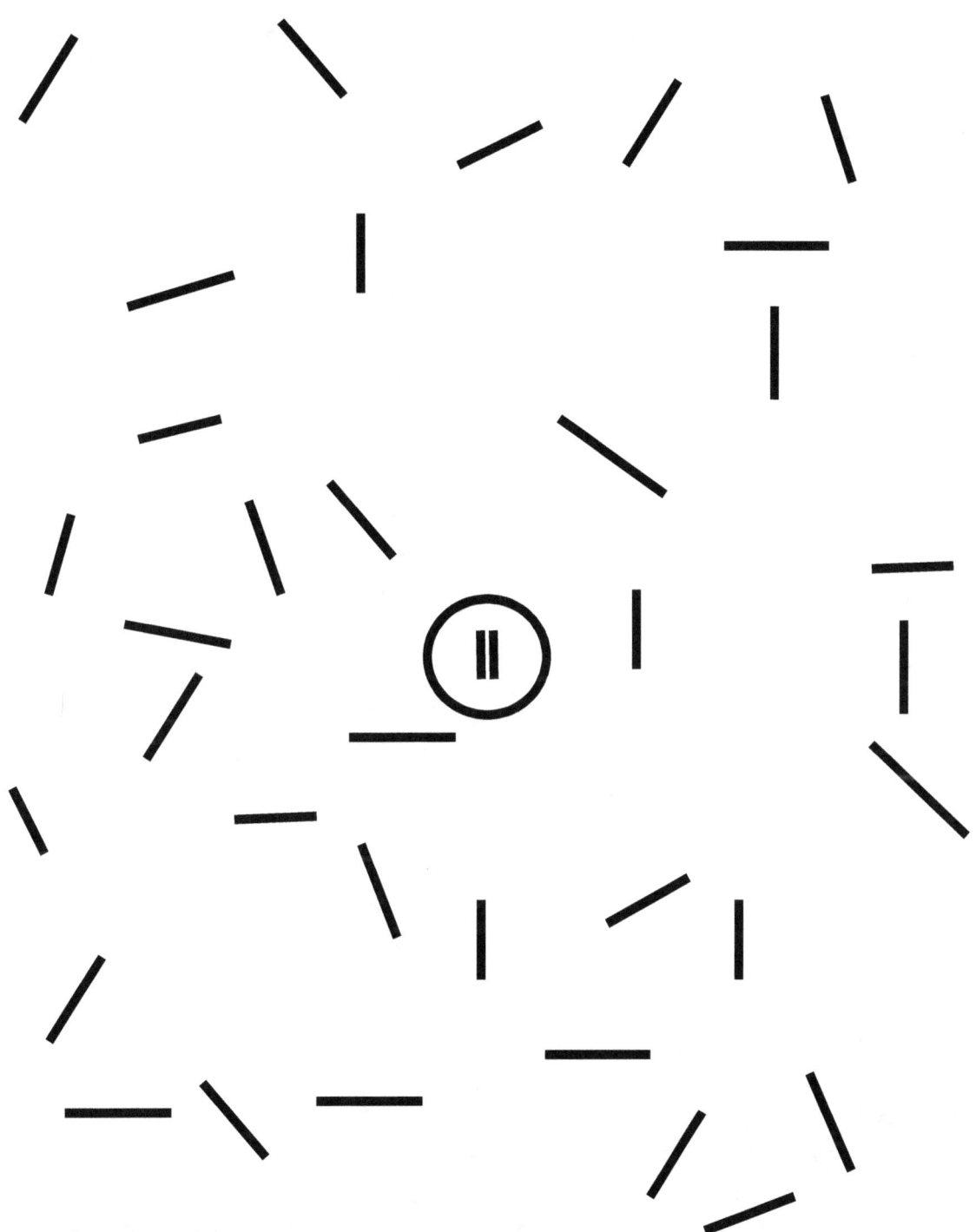

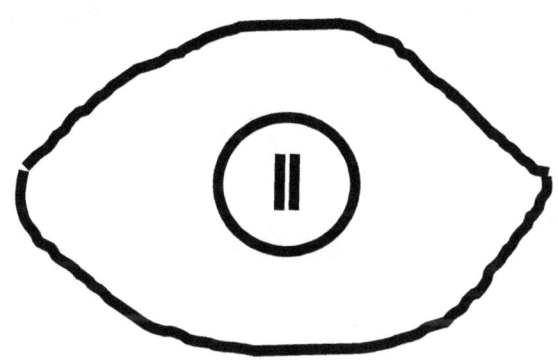

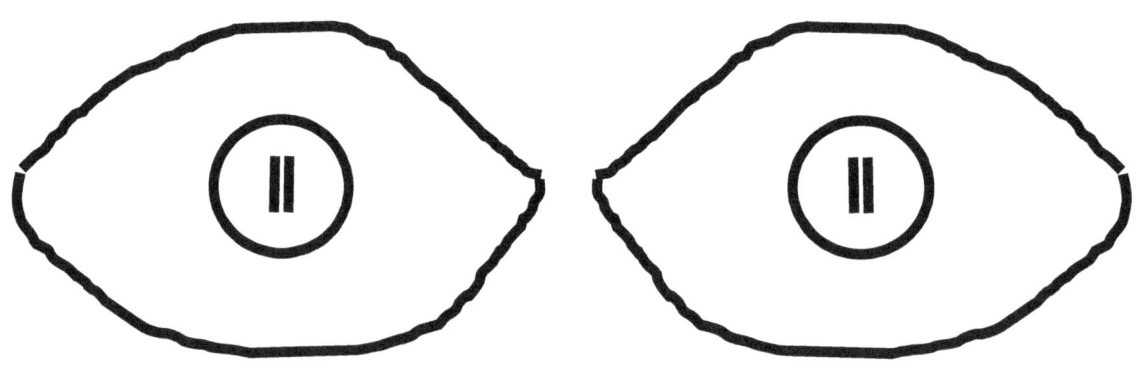

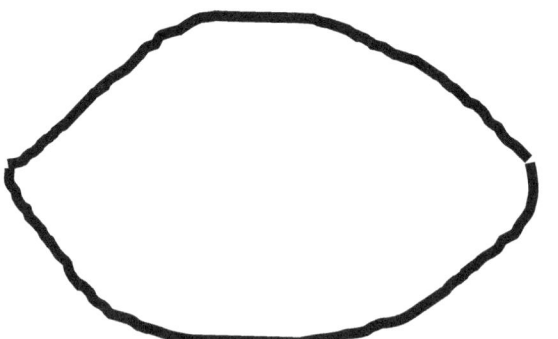

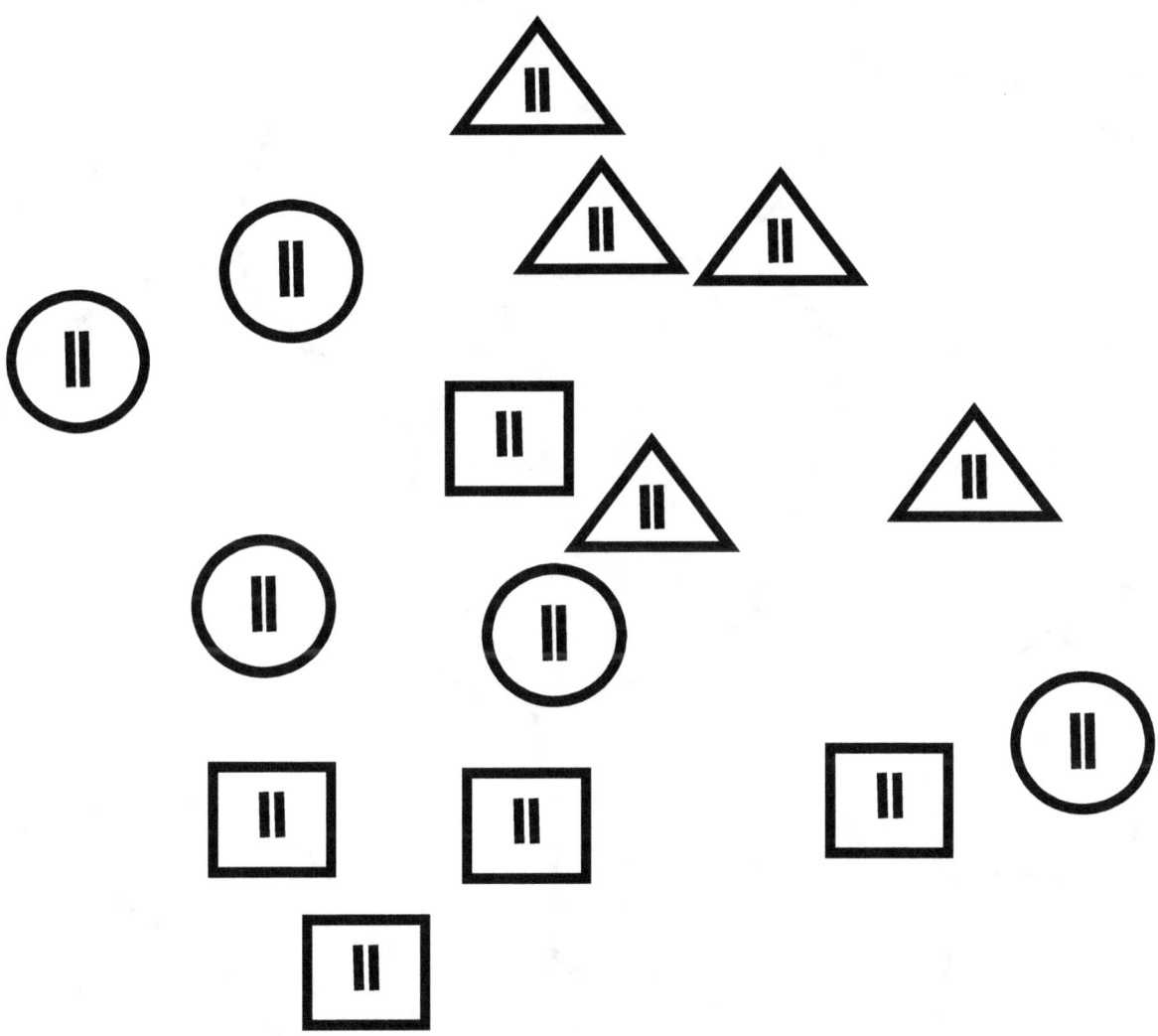

81

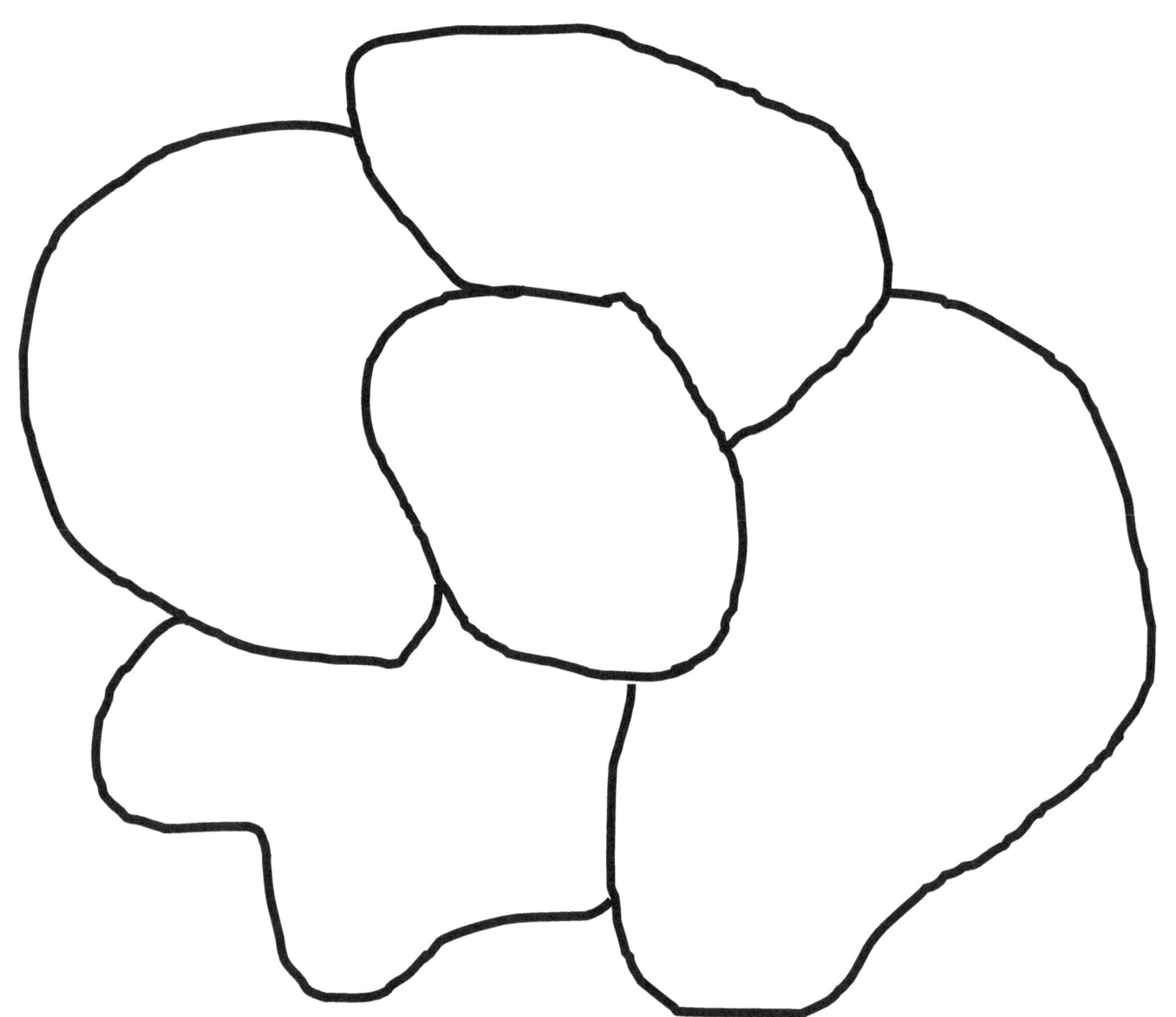

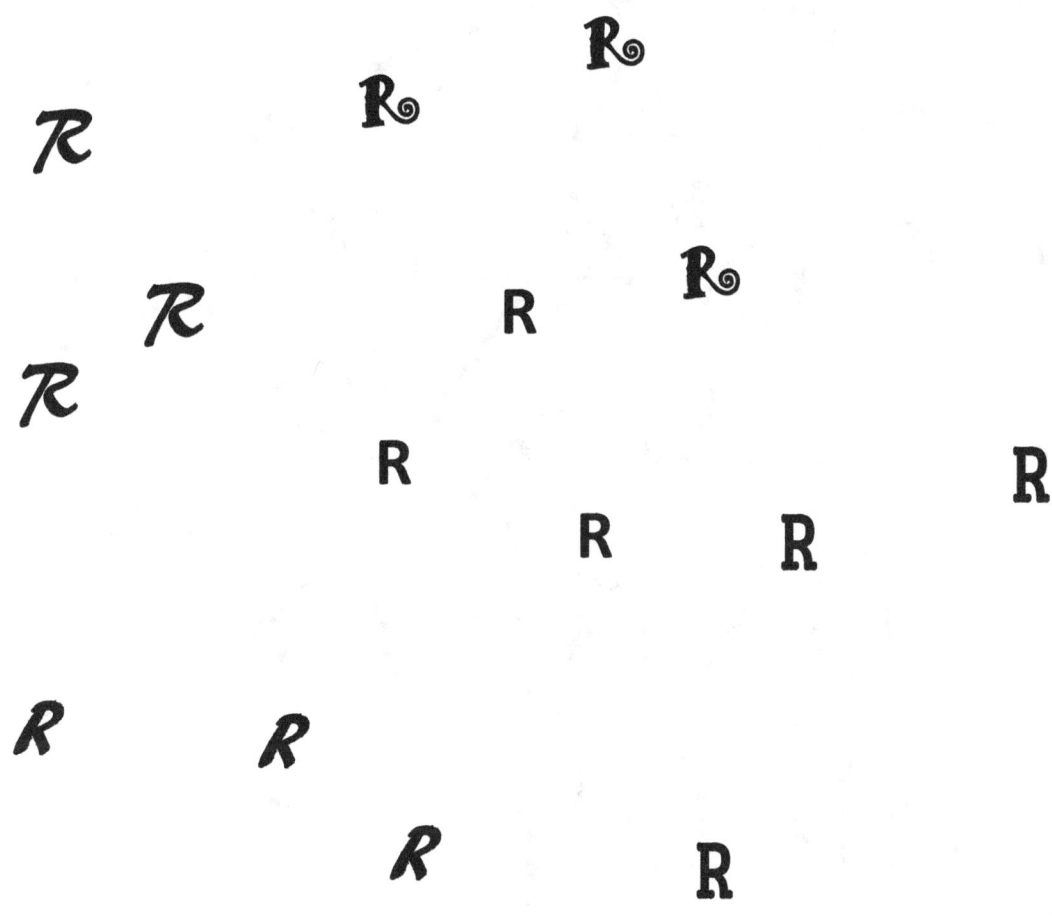

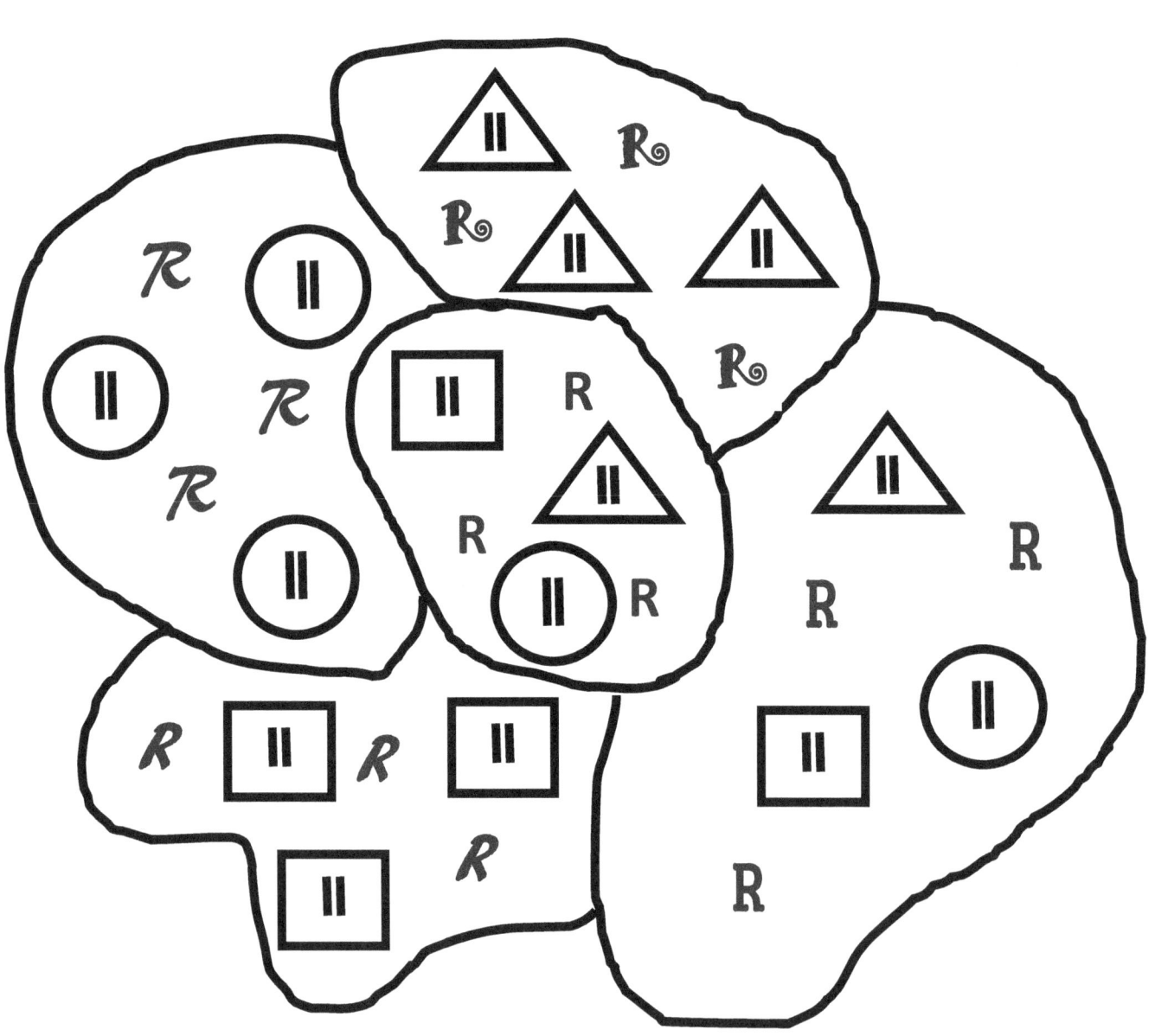

SONGS
IN THE
KEY
OF
SEE

Table of Some Contents

Meaning and Morality...12

The Individual...12

Liberty and Equality...13

These Songs...13

Pictures...14

If I Found...16

Blind Men at Work...17

Mediocre Town...20

Pretty Little Angel...24

Cultural Prescription...26

Ol' John Henry...28

Not Something I Saw...30

The Establishment...36

Gliding on a Rainbow...40

Georgie...42

Loyal Disrespect...44

Her Sweet Shoulder...46

Language...48

Propositions...48

Table of Some Contents

Questions...53

Distinct Concepts...55

Key Questions...55

Paradox...59

Social Systems...60

Propaganda...60

Logic and Reality...60

Poorly Differentiated Concepts...62

The Resurrection of Meaning and Morality...62

Songs

If I Found
Blind Men at Work
Mediocre Town
Pretty Little Angel
Cultural Prescription
Ol' John Henry
Not Something I Saw
The Establishment
Gliding on a Rainbow
Georgie
Loyal Disrespect
Her Sweet Shoulder

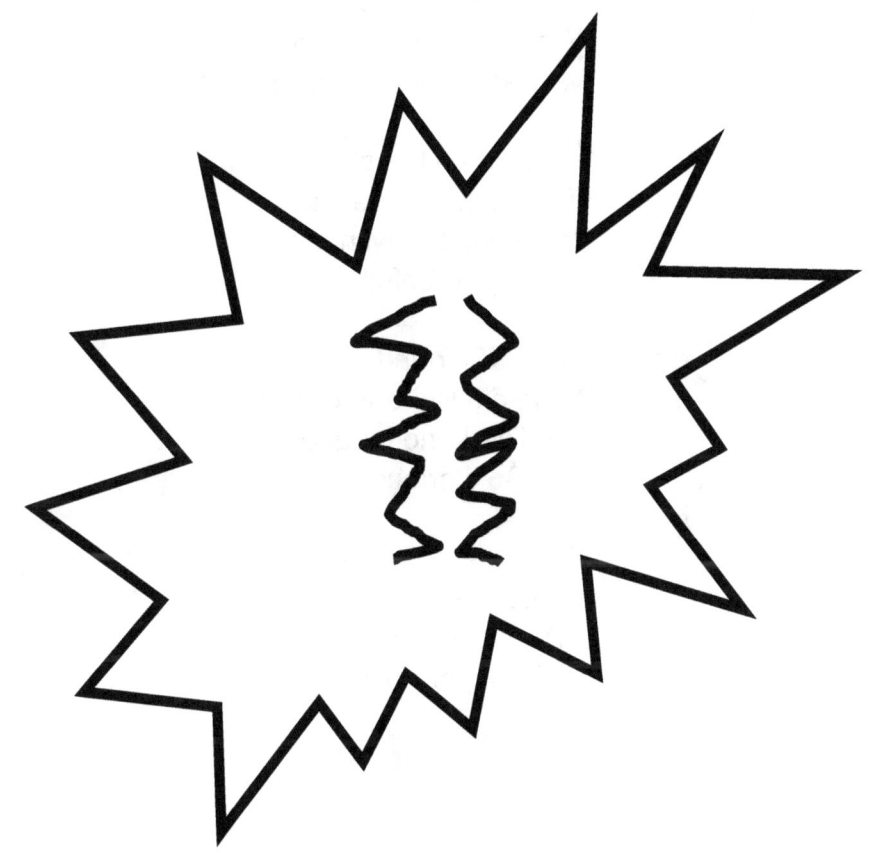

If I Found

If I found her
Who thought like that
Would walk and talk and felt like that

Alive as the sky
And deep as the sea
Would wander with time
So gracefully

If I found
That she did live and breathe
And lived and laughed
So gloriously

Would that be love?
Would that be me?
And would we live
Separately

Blind Men at Work

There are blind men at work
Working every day
Working minutes, hours
Working for good pay.

There are blind men at work
At jobs that require sight
Laughing away the daytime
And wasting time at night.

Their cause is a noble one
And they all have good hearts
But even working hard
They'll only do a part.

'Cause they're blind men.
Blind men.

Can't work in this world
On things that you just don't see
Can't work on answers
To questions unknown to me.

Can't work with the future
Until it's made known
Can't work with time
Until you feel it growing.

There are blind men at work
Workin' oh so hard
Let's give them something
So we all can do our part.

Mediocre Town

In a mediocre town
Filled with mediocre men
Playing mediocre games
With mediocre friends

Live some mediocre guys
With mediocre eyes
Telling mediocre lies
Over mediocre fries.

Dating mediocre gals
Making mediocre vows
Raising mediocre kids
And families.

Live in mediocre homes
On mediocre streets
Lined by mediocre shrubs
And mediocre trees.

Mediocre rooms
With mediocre floors
Mediocre windows
And mediocre doors.

Mediocre walls
Mediocre halls
Mediocre cellphones
And mediocre calls.

Driving mediocre vans
Getting mediocre tans
Mediocre toys and candies

Mediocre schools
Mediocre rules
Mediocre songs
'Bout where we all belong.

Mediocre good deeds
And mediocre sins
Mediocre losses
And mediocre wins.

Mediocre smiles
Mediocre frowns
Mediocre caps
And mediocre gowns.

Mediocre feeling
Mediocre thought
Mediocre things
That were just bought.

Then comes a noble, young soul
With higher goals
Looking for something
That just ain't sold.

Looks over here
Looks over there
Looking and looking everywhere.

In this mediocre town
Filled with mediocre men
Playing mediocre jokes
On mediocre friends

Mediocre guys
With mediocre eyes
Telling mediocre lies
Over hot apple pie.

Pretty Little Angel

I had a pretty little angel
I had a pretty little angel
She stepped out of a dream
Walked into my life
Stepped out of a dream.

I had a pretty little angel
I had a pretty little angel
She walked into my life
Stepped out of a dream
Walked into my life.

Now she means so much to me
Means so much to me
Means so much to me
Yes she does
She always seems to make me
Smile, smile, smile
Oh, yes, she does
And she will.

Now she's come and gone
She's far from home
Gone, gone, gone, gone

Now she's on her own and
Roams, roams, roams
In her own home.

I had a pretty little angel
I had a pretty little angel
He stepped out of a dream
Walked into my life
Stepped out of a dream.

I had a pretty little angel
I had a pretty little angel
He walked into my life
Stepped out of a dream
Walked into my life.

Now he means so much to me
Means so much to me
Means so much to me
Yes he does
He always seems to make me
Smile, smile, smile
Oh, yes, he does
And he will.

Now he's come and gone
He's far from home
Gone, gone, gone, gone

Now he's on his own and
Roams, roams, roams
In his own home.

Cultural Prescription

Well the gang's all down
At the local corner parlor
Laughing with each other
'Bout the local food and barber

Some new folk walk in
From a little further farther
Need something more
Need something strong
Need to feel a life
Where we all belong

Need a cultural prescription
Need to feel about something
We all can believe in
A spirit of life
We all live alive with
Need a cultural prescription
Need a cultural prescription.

Well the gang's all down
At the local corner parlor
Laughing with each other
'Bout the local food and barber

Some new folk walk in
From a little further farther
Need something more
Need something strong
Need to feel a life
Where we all belong

Need a cultural prescription
Need to feel about something
We all can agree on
A spirit of life
We all live alive with

Need a cultural prescription
Cultural prescription.

Ol' John Henry

Ol' John Henry
Had gone to school
Ostensibly to learn
But his mind had been abused

That school was good
This John knew
But to learn to think
Meant breaking some rules.

So there John sat
With his philosophy
And while his teachers taught facts
John sought meaning

General propositions
He for sure wanted to know
But it was the framework of thought
That he wondered about.
And he thought.

Simple minded people
They do simple minded things
All day.
All day, all day, all day.
All day, all day.

Simple minded people
They do simple minded things
All day.
All day, all day, all day.
All day, all day.

Show me a simple man
And I'll show you a simple way.

Not Something I Saw

It's not something I saw
On my trip to the West
Although it was going on all the time
Without rest.

Nothing was said
And nothing was seen
But the eyes that all passed
Knew it to be.

It goes on all the time
It's always with us
But the most we seem to do
Is pet it, when it begs us.

For finding meaning
We're at a loss
'Cause the questions people asking
Misplace the force.

Meaning is nothing
Intrinsic to thee
It's just how we group things
It's relations we see.

I saw it all the time
In misguided expression
Confused and abused
Not knowing any better.

Not many of those things
Were seen by these eyes
Except in small bits
Of imaginative play
But it goes on all the time.
All the time, all the time, all the time.

To put one against another
With such shallow symbols
Keeps expression misguided
And always kept hiding.

The Establishment

The establishment
Of kinds and classes
That making do require
Some kind of easy,
Recognizable mark
'Cause that what membership desire.

You feel silly
You're not like that
And you want to make amends.
You feel guilty
You don't make it
Inside either end.

But that don't mean
There is no room
It don't mean
You can't be.

It just mean
The world around
Oh, it's just not like
You or me.

Oh, what I see
And what I feel
It's just not
Like that.

And you can't
Tell me
That that's all there is
And all there is is fact.

Gliding on a Rainbow

I'm gliding on a rainbow
Down toward heaven on earth
She is a woman
And I've loved her since birth.

I am a man
If you must know
And our children wander near and far
In our happy home.

Life is so pretty here
Sometimes I think I might cry
And whenever I feel the urge coming on
Oh, she's right here by my side.

Happiness comes in all different colors
In all the ways we're related to each other

I'm gliding on a rainbow
Down toward heaven on earth
She is a woman and I'm a man
And we've loved each other since birth.

Georgie

Georgie, Georgie
When will you be happy?
Georgie, Georgie
When will you not blame?

Georgie, Georgie
When will you see reality?
Georgie, Georgie
When will you be sane?

I know you just want to
Love the one you're with
I know you just want to
Be loved and forgiven.

Georgie, Georgie
When will you be happy?
I know you just cannot
Feel love or forgive.

Loyal Disrespect

He's got loyal disrespect for his family
He's got loyal disrespect for his friends
He's got loyal disrespect for his lover
He's got loyal disrespect 'til the end

He's got loyal disrespect for his brother
He's got loyal disrespect for his son
He's got loyal disrespect for his man in the street
He's so lousy he won't respect no one.

Now he sits there thinks he's so charming
Sits there acting so cool
Sits there feels he's so graceful
But he sit and break all the rules

Now the man seem to hide his feeling
So that nothing seem to make much sense
He'll smile when he thinking you ugly
And he'll laugh when he wish you was dead.

She's got loyal disrespect for her family
She's got loyal disrespect for her friends
She's got loyal disrespect for her lover
She's got loyal disrespect 'til the end

She's got loyal disrespect for her brother
She's got loyal disrespect for her son
She's got loyal disrespect for his woman in the street
She's so lousy she won't respect no one.

Now she sits there thinks she's so charming
Sits there acting so cool
Sits there feels she's so graceful
But she sit and break all the rules

Now the woman seem to hide her feeling
So that nothing seem to make much sense
She'll smile when she thinking you ugly
And she'll laugh when she wish you was dead.

Loyal disrespect.

Her Sweet Shoulder

I cried on her sweet
shoulder
She held me close to
her
I knew not what I did
But said: Take me as I
am.

I cried on her sweet
shoulder
She held me tight and
warm
A glimpse of feeling
naked
Will you take me as I
am?

She held me close
against her
Cradled in her hands
She knew not what she
did
But said: I love you as
you stand.

I cried on her sweet
shoulder
She held me close to
her
I knew not what I did
But said: Take me as I
am.

I love to be the best to
her
I thought that is what
love did mean
Being what she needs
Is all I meant to be.

And being true to myself
I thought I could have
both
Then a spirit came
surging through
And said: Take me as I
am.

I cried on her sweet
shoulder
She held me tight and
warm
A glimpse of feeling
naked
Will you take me as I
am?

She held me close
against her
Cradled in her hands
She knew not what she
did
But said: I love you as
you stand.

I cried on her sweet
shoulder
I want her oh so bad
You are the only one
who knows me deep
You are the only one I
have

There are some things
only time will give
Given two spirits that
flow free
To meet and greet and
want each other
Two spirits, you and me.

I cried on her sweet
shoulder
She held me close to
her
I knew not what I did
But said: Take me as I
am.

I cried on her sweet
shoulder
I knew not what I did
But said take me as I
am Sweet Love
And that's just what
Love did give.

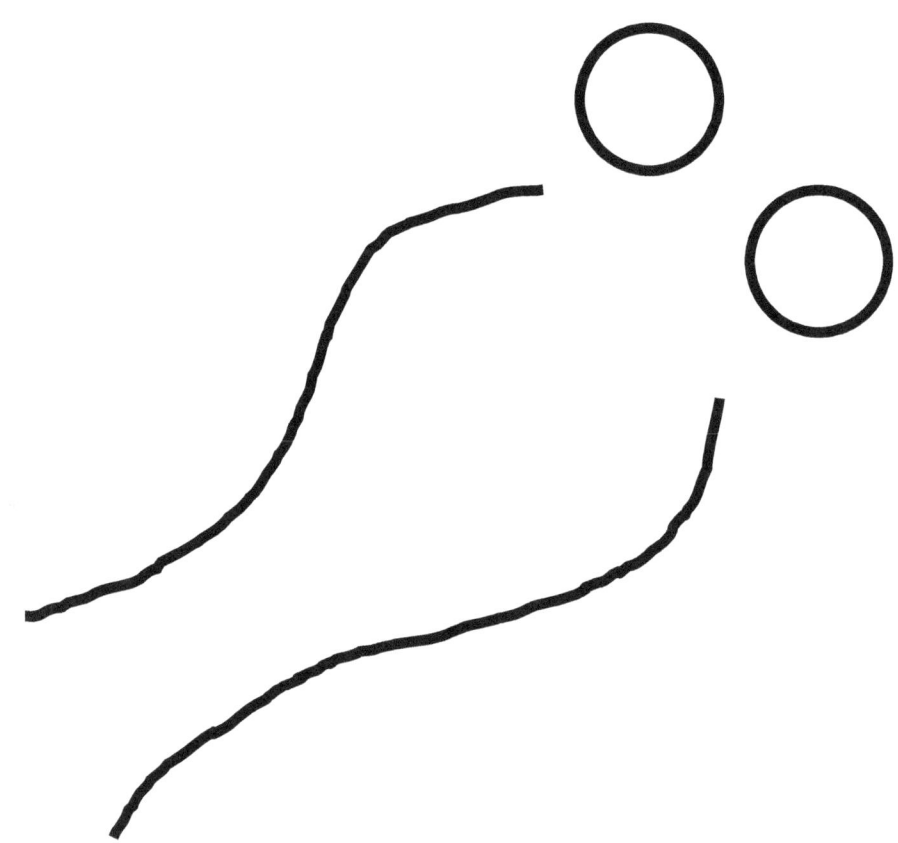

Address correspondence to: Logical Arts Press at L.A.PRESS8@gmail.com